The Norfolk and Norwich
World Family

The largest "family" of interrelated communities
in the world

The plaque presented to those communities present
at the First World Gathering

The Norfolk and Norwich World Family

Derek Bickford-Smith

with contributions from
Ian Smith, Helen Hoyte, Ruby Mogard, Mary Lindbo, David Crisp,
Karlene Skillen, Dorothy Peck, Thelma Ravinski, Betsy Pine,
Geri Tasker, Mary Clark, Kathryn Barton, Janet Decker,
John and Doris Allen, Carlyn Seighman, Patricia Fay, Ross Porter,
Peggy Hale McPhillips, Richard Ivy, Alastair Honeybun,
Hazel Cook, Wendy Robyn, Clare Tarr, Nadine Dobbin,
Elva McLean, Jo Watson, Ian Hamilton McCowan
and many other wonderful people

Designer and Editor – Ken Ward
Cover design – Coralie Bickford-Smith

First published 2004
by The Norfolk and Norwich World Family
12 Chapelfield North, Norwich NR2 1NY, Norfolk, UK

British Library Cataloguing in Publication Data
A catalogue record for this book is available from the British Library

ISBN 0-9547615-0-2

Printed and bound in Malta

Definition

A Community: A body of people that have a named place (district) in terms of common residence and organisation … that which is accepted as such and so named by the overall administration.

Contents

About the Author	xi
Foreword	xiii
Acknowledgements	xv
Editor's Notes	xvii
Aims of the Norfolk and Norwich Gathering	1
Finding 'The Family'	5
Requiem for the Lost Norfolk and Norwich Communities	9
The First World Family Gathering	13
The Second World Family Gathering	19
Future "Family Gatherings"	25

The "Family"

United Kingdom
England	27
The Early Emigrations	28
Norfolk Textiles	31
Norfolk County, England	34
Norfolk County Council	36
District councils:	
King's Lynn and West Norfolk	38
North Norfolk	40
Broadland	42
Great Yarmouth	44
South Norfolk	46
Breckland	48
Norwich City, Norfolk County, England	50
HMS Norfolk	57

United States of America
Connecticut	59
Norwich City, CT	60
Norfolk Town, CT	68

West Norfolk, CT 75
South Norfolk, CT 75
Dakota 76
    Norwich, Minot, ND 77
Iowa 80
    Norwich, Shenandoah, IA 81
Kansas 84
    Norwich City, KA 85
Massachusetts 90
    Norfolk County, MA 91
    Norfolk Town, MA 96
    Norfolk Downs, Quincy, MA 100
    Norwich, MA 102
Michigan 104
    Norwich Township, Missaukee, MI 105
    Norwich Township, Newaygo, MI 108
Minnesota 110
    Norfolk Township, MN 111
Nebraska 113
    Norfolk City, NE 114
New York 118
    Norwich City and Norwich Town, NY 119
    North Norwich, NY 124
    East Norwich, NY 127
    Norwich Corners, NY 132
    Norfolk, NY 133
Ohio 140
    Norwich Township, Franklin, OH 141
    Norwich Township, Huron, OH 144
    Norwich Village, Muskingum, OH 146
Pennsylvania 148
    Norwich Township, PA 149
    Norwich, PA 151
Vermont 154
    Norwich, VT 155
    West Norwich, VT 159
    Norwich University, VT 160

Virginia   161
    Norfolk City, VA   162
    Norfolk State University, Norfolk ,VA   167
    South Norfolk, Chesapeake, VA   168
    Norfolk Highlands, Chesapeake, VA   170
    Port Norfolk, Portsmouth, VA   171
    West Norfolk, Portsmouth, VA   174
USS Norfolk   175

Australia
Western Australia   177
    Norfolk Estate, Quinns Rocks   178
Tasmania   181
    New Norfolk   182
Norfolk Island   186

Canada
Manitoba   193
    Municipality of North Norfolk   194
    Municipality of South Norfolk   198
Ontario   201
    Norfolk County   202
    Norfolk Township   205
    Norwich Township, Oxford County   207
    Norwich Village, Oxford County   208

Jamaica
Jamaica   211
    Norwich and Norwich Halt, Surrey County   212
    Norwich, Middlesex County   213
    Norfolk, Cornwall County   213

New Zealand
North Island   215
    Norfolk, Taranaki, New Plymouth   216

About the Author

Derek Bickford-Smith was born in Pernambuco, Brazil while his father was working on building the railway, then reared on the family farm in Sussex, England. Educated at Ardingly and Steyning Grammar School. Served in the Indian Army (the Kumaon Regiment) just prior to Indian Independence and thence to the British Army (King's Own Royal Regiment), serving in Cyprus, Palestine and North Africa.

After studying at Shuttleworth Agricultural College he became a farm manager, and then an agricultural advisor with a national company for some 30 years, working first in Yorkshire and Durham and later in Norfolk, Suffolk and Cambridgeshire. As one of his side interests, Derek organised farm exchange delegations via the National Embassies of China, Russia, Romania, Bulgaria, East Germany and West Germany, Poland, Hungary and Turkey; as well as farmer visits to Ireland, France, Italy, South Africa, Ethiopia, Kenya, Israel and New Zealand.

Since retirement Derek has become a tourist guide to Norwich City, plus being a local coordinator to that excellent world friendship organisation SERVAS.

In 1991, he was co-opted by Norwich City to be the Assistant Regalia Curator to Stanley Taylor and thence the realisation that with the inherent "world globalisation", Norfolk and Norwich ought to get into the act.

This has led to the discovery of those world communities, unknown to each other, with Norfolk or Norwich in their address and their becoming the largest such "family" in the world.

It has also led to finding that there are over 2,000 place, business and family names Norfolk or Norwich in the world.

There are approaching 3 million people in our world who have the community address Norfolk or Norwich.

Derek has either visited or travelled very near to all but four of the 53 communities so indexed and given some 60 talks plus radio interviews and written press articles on his own English communities, at most of which the question was "Where is Norfolk or Norwich in England?" let alone their own neighbours. He lives in the original Norwich in Norfolk, which however indirectly, have been the progenitors of all others.

Derek and Huguette embarking on one of their many travels

Foreword

In each community I have discovered friends, and with the fabulous help of the librarians of the world I have begun the information trail that has led to each of the mentioned communities. If there be one international statistic then it is the fact that our ladies have been the ones with the vision to recognise the potential of this research and it is really to them that this family is dedicated! 99% of my helpers have been these wonderful people.

The internet has given vent to this opportunity and the facilities offered by the search engines such as Google mean that web site complexities are largely sorted out for me – just type in a word and it is all there!

This has been a labour of love and a small contribution to the peace of the world.

ONCE WE GET TO KNOW ONE ANOTHER,
WE UNDERSTAND, WE CAN TALK,
AND THE NEED FOR FIGHTING IS VASTLY LESSENED!

Derek Bickford-Smith
At home in Norwich, Norfolk UK
January 2004

Acknowledgements

So many people have helped turn The Norfolk and Norwich World Family into a reality. The complete list would be a book on its own, but I feel I must mention the generosity of Simon Gurney and his excellent friendly company at www.netcom.co.uk for the computer and internet facilities.

Probably the most impressive of our presentations to date was that of the first ever gathering of the World Norfolk and Norwich communities in Norwich, Norfolk, UK, and that memory was confirmed by our CEO of public relations, namely Julian Foster with his marathon of photography. Thanks to him we appreciate the importance of picture stories.

Information and enthusiasm have come from all communities and to choose but a few... the help of Marian O'Keefe (coordinator North America) has been outstanding, and in no order of merit... Vicky Brothers (Norfolk NY), Louise Schimmel (Norfolk CT), Clare Tarr (North Norfolk Manitoba), Marge Chomyszak, George M. Sands IV (Norwich NY), Dorothy Horton McGee (East Norwich NY), John and Jean Lawe (Norwich VT), Margaret Tumicki (Norwich CT), William O'Donnell and Henry Ainslie (Norfolk County MA), the ever bubbling Pearl and Nadine Dobbin and their English partner in support, John Leader (South Norfolk Manitoba), Lance and Jacqueline Body (Norwich Village, Oxford Ontario), Jackie Whitehead and Damian Bester (New Norfolk, Tasmania), Agnes Hain, Tom Lloyd, Gillian Reckitt, Allan Kerr, Angela Guymer, Nan and Fred Smith and many more (Norfolk Island), Harley Rector (Norfolk Nebraska), Breck Daughtrey the strength of Norfolk VA, Karlene and Jim Skillen (Norwich Kansas), Joyce and Bob Wilson (Norfolk NZ), Sir Timothy Colman, Lord Lieutenant to Norfolk County UK (who attended all our main functions in his county), His Grace the recent Duke of Norfolk, Pauline Denzey (Norfolk County Council, UK), Mary E. Baruth (Manager Heritage & Culture Division Norfolk County Ontario), Karen Matthews (Manager Norfolk County Fair Ontario), Sheree Leeds (coord. UK), Mary Ryder, Jim and June Marriage, the Museum and Norwich societies (all of Norwich City

UK), Margaret Ince, who from the outset made sure this would be done! Pippa Bastin, who gave me that first colourful spread in her Norfolk Journal, and so many more recognisers of this immense potential for inter-communication. All those hundreds of librarians without whom we would have not progressed at all, and the few schools who have grasped the opportunity.

A sincere thanks to the Eastern Daily Press and the Norwich (UK) Evening News for their constant promotion of the imprtance to Norfolk and Norwich of the largest "family" in the world.

Finally, but by no means least, my thanks to Ken Ward. Without his dedication this book would never have been realised.

In 15 years of research, travel, letters and e-mails, I have missed out so very many here, but none the less recollection brings warm feeling of friendship for this, the largest "family of namesake communities" in the world (not to mention those Norfolk and Norwich place names that bespeak past peoples and are now but memories – some thousands).

So, how did it all come about? Well, that is real history to be researched by another.... In the meantime, this book is a record of the discoveries so far and my early travels to meet all those wonderful people.

Material for the book has come from so many sources. We have where possible acknowledged them. For any we have missed please accept my sincere apologies.

It is hoped that this book will encourage others to contribute information and photographs for future editions which will be published on the Norfolk and Norwich Family web site at www. gurney.co.uk/norfolk/

In gratitude for this opportunity to communicate!
Your servant, Derek

Editor's Notes

In the course of compiling this book, a problem has arisen over the terms used in the countries involved. The language in all may be English, but the same word doesn't necessarily mean the same thing in other countries, so a brief explanation is required.

UK	County	District	Town/City	Village/Parish
U.S.A. State	County	Township	Town/City	Village
Canada	Province/ Territory	Municipality	Town/City	Village
Australia	State	Shire?	Town/City	Village
New Zealand	Region	District	Town/City	Village
Jamaica	County	Parish	Town/City	Village

With the US entries, there has been confusion because (to take a worst case scenario) there can be a city, town, township and village all with the same name in the same location, and documents just refer to the name (Norwich or Norfolk) without clarifying which. Also, in the U.S.A. many of the counties, towns, etc. have been renamed over the years.

So if you, dear reader, find any mistakes in this book, please forgive us and let us know.

This book is dedicated to our World Family whose existence would never have been realised but for Stanley Taylor and his City of Norwich Regalia, the finest and oldest in the world.
And to the people whom I have met that will always give me hope, faith, vision and laughter …

WORLD FAMILY
www.gurney.co.uk/norfolk
Norfolk   Norwich

Aims of
the Norfolk and Norwich Gathering
(with comments)

An unique "family"

- There are no language problems although the customs of each are interestingly different (even within the North American communities!).

- Each community has a very limited knowledge of its "relations"!

- Every community is related, however remotely, to the original Norfolk and Norwich.

- This is the largest "namesake community family" in the world.

- Many communities have now been visited with talks being given on our original Norfolk and Norwich in England, and understandably the inevitable question has been "Where is the English Norwich and where is the English Norfolk?" – as indeed in England the same question has been asked concerning our overseas "relatives!"

The aims of the founder members

- To hold gatherings every few years based upon a different Family Community.

- To provide information and contacts within each community for visitors from other namesake communities. It is wonderful how, now that introductions have been made, every community is extremely keen to be allowed to welcome visitors from others of their "family".

It is hoped that this will continue to expand by:-

1. Schools using e-mail to contact and inform each other of themselves. Item:- The most remarkable fact is that schools spend an important part of the education time teaching a foreign language and yet their pupils in the main forget this as soon as they leave.
Here, in the Norfolk and Norwich World Family contacts, we have the facility that needs no preparation and yet schools are, again in the main, reluctant to add this potential as a part of life's education via that much heralded e-mail cum internet.

2. Associations contacting and exchanging information, the Lions, Rotary, Masons, St John's Ambulance, Salvation Army, British Legion, etc. The reality of such interchange is yet to be realised.

3. Libraries exchanging informative books. Librarians are the world's best co-informants and the statistics show that our future on such a scene is in the hands of the ladies with that vision that seems to be uniquely theirs.

4. Local authorities maintaining such information of potential world connections so that their own peoples can take advantage via the individual tourist offices.

5. The collection of the histories of each community is gradually being amassed and these will be edited into one publication for distribution to each community's library and local authority.

6. Our "Norfolk and Norwich Gathering" web site is aimed to be the focal point where each community will be enabled to put reference to its own web sites, those of its area, its schools, churches, libraries and associations, thus making another ongoing and updated connection. Web sites are only effective if an exchange of references is made and here is a central point for effectiveness!

Help in all these aims can be obtained by e-mailing Derek Bickford-Smith on dimsmith@netcom.co.uk.

The potential for education and "getting to know" each other is one of the main contributions toward peace in our world.

This potential has been wonderfully started by those of each community who are contributing with vision and confidence ... the statistics are a compliment to the ladies in that 99% of those have been our contributing founder members!

Finding "The Family"
The beginnings and wanderings

The initiative for the start of this research for Norfolks and Norwiches around the world was the visitor book started by Stanley Taylor in his uniquely organised City Regalia Exhibition in 1991 – a book signed by visitors from all over the world during the five years of that exhibition. Since the time of Stanley's residence the regalia has largely been lost to the public and is now housed, impersonally and without the fascinating background that Stanley used to describe to his many visitors. A regalia without peer in the United Kingdom (and the world!). Even that of the City of London was largely destroyed during that original Cromwellian revolution.

Left: Stanley W. Taylor – that true Norfolk and Norwich gentleman – unassuming, but with oh so many stories and an immense sense of humour!

Stanley Taylor's record:

31 years of service to Norwich City Council.
16 years Mace Bearer – Toastmaster etc.
11 years Chauffeur to the Lord Mayor.
3 years City Regalia Curator.
He served 72 City dignitaries – Lord Mayors and Sheriffs. Took part in 23,000 civic engagements, and more!
And before that — awkward squad Army service, fearless steel erector everywhere – on his motor bike!
A FANTASTIC MAN!!!

The visitors book in Stanley's Regalia exhibition contained the record of 10 Norfolk and Norwich communities.

The astonishment at that time was how little was known of Norfolk & Norwich namesakes – Norwich Union records showed but a few. Norwich City and Norfolk County knew no more, and the American resources were no help in that first instance.

Finally it was through large scale maps that primary discoveries were made, written to and in many cases eliciting no interest or replies. The realisation came that the only way to make progress was to visit, invited or not. The discovery of being able to become a courier, with minimal fare costs, within the constraints of having two weeks between the outgoing and the return journey meant that it all became economically possible.

That first series of visits was with the seven communities who had been kind enough to respond to my self invitation. Each gave facilities for talks, radio broadcasts and press reporting, so that the baggage of literature was in several pieces of luggage and my arrival at Kennedy airport was beset with carriage difficulties.

A large dark form hung over me and said "Can I carry your bags?" – so despite my nervousness in that by then empty airport I agreed. We arrived at the bus stop for my hired car station and I only had a $10 bill and despite my helper saying that he would go and get some change I waved this goodbye. However when the bus arrived I was welcomed by my porter with that change! Quite the warmest welcome I had ever had to any country!

Car hire was a foreign language as was the automatic car, as I attempted to find the way out of New York toward Connecticut and my first Norwich community. In becoming lost early on, I stopped at a hot-dog stand and asked a lorry driver for help. He turned to a friend to chat, then turned back to me and said in that "foreign" English, "Come in between us and we will put you on the right road". And so this tiny little red car went between the two motoring monstrosities onto the highway and was honked off onto the correct road.

The chapter of experiences continued at a bridge toll where in my confusion I gave $10 instead of $1 and heard the cry from the attendant "10 dollars!", by which time it was too late in that stream of concentrated traffic. Those dollar notes looked so much alike!

The sight of that first road sign "NORWICH" meant a photographic session. I couldn't find the hand brake, so left my car in the lowest of gears on an upgrade, took my photograph and turned round to find the car gently coming toward me. I put my foot out to stop the wheel, only to find that when it did stop it had run over my foot! To be sitting on the side of the road run over by one's own car was ridiculous in the extreme! I managed to get my foot out of the shoe and turn off the engine. So glad I was on my own!

Every journey had its own story and those specifically related to a community are shown on the appropriate pages. However my second series of visits had its separate adventure in that I discovered that I had been awake for 36 hours and still driving to my first call! Immediately I felt tired, it was a lovely sunny day, so I pulled in and walked into a field and went to sleep. Woke up refreshed and went to the car and realised that I couldn't hear the engine. I should say that I was and am almost stone deaf without my hearing aids – there was disaster before I had begun! But luck was with me as I remembered admiring a clump of weed in that field where I had laid down and there was my tiny hearing aid....

Just one more separate incident of so many. On my third series of visits, having flown late at night, squeezed by an overweight man who took half my seat as well as his own, from Ontario to New York for onward to Virginia; I had to spend the night and had booked an

hotel at the airport, only to find that despite this, my hotel had gone out of existence. I taxied into New York and tried to find a hotel that I had stayed in before with no success and was dumped by my taxi driver in the belief that the YMCA was nearby – but where?
There were two very large dark gentlemen lying on the pavement and one slowly unwound and came over to me and asked the time.
I was terrified but complied, and his reply was that there was no point in going home at 2 a.m. He rejoined his companion on the pavement. However, he knew of the YMCA and even at that early morning hour I was welcomed to that excellent establishment.

What were further happenings? In the 62 talks, five radio interviews and countless newspaper mentions whilst travelling more than twice round the world? We shall see when visiting each community in the following pages....

WORLD FAMILY
www.gurney.co.uk/norfolk

Norfolk   Norwich

Requiem for the Lost
Norfolk and Norwich Communities
by Derek Bickford-Smith

Today's 2.5 million residents – rising 3 million – who comprise the
existing Norfolk and Norwich communities bear witness to those
previous communities subsumed by events such as climate and
economics, and even sheer grasping for power by their neighbours.
There are so very many questions in the case of each of these
deceased communities – How? Why? When? And it is hoped that
by registering them here, there will be friends who will come forth
to fill in the detail. Such lost communities are almost totally within
the United States of America. The whole question of American
history would seem to be bound up with the immense dislocation of
the disastrous civil war. So many young men went to battle and lost
their lives, with the result that much of their original background was
destroyed.

The remarkable ghost town of Norwich, Pennsylvania – where the
vestiges have been turned into an historical site. Here was a thriving
community based upon the extraction of timber, but that was an
expendable commodity.

The next State of Virginia, namely that area which is one vast
conurbation now divided between Norfolk, Chesapeake and
Portsmouth, was a proud possessor of Norfolk Heights and West
Norfolk whilst South Norfolk has been accepted by a community
to be remembered by the Chesapeake authorities. My attempts to
re-identify them were negatived as "no longer being in existence",
but, as will be seen they are still very much alive under that new
administration.

Mississippi and Missouri States with their lost Norfolk communities that became areas for flood relief for that vast lifeline river – can one imagine the first delight at discovering lush pastures only to be "outed" in the name of progress? All this information delightfully conveyed by librarian Shirley Briant. Her acceptance of one of our "family" pins was charming.

New York State with its four Norwiches – City, Town, North and East – still there were yet more Norwiches which seem to have been in existence until the late 1890s but are now so vaguely remembered in the library records.

Norfolk, Connecticut – a most charming almost holiday town with a barely existing South Norfolk, deprecated as being of no importance and a bare West Norfolk graveyard that shows hitherto pride in Polish ancestry.

Vermont with a seeming West Norwich in two places, but the one having the most poignant graveyard that I have ever visited. The crosses and slate headstones on that lonely hillside bearing recognition to those who had laid down their farming tools to decamp to Boston, so very many walking miles away, and fight with enthusiasm for a conceived freedom, only to lose their lives so far away. And their loved ones, bringing their bodies back, again so many walking miles, to this hillside. Remembered now by the headstones and crosses marked 1776.

Georgia and map memories of Norfolk – a post office in an unmapped area where the community became redundant. Hardly even in memory, save for the researches of Susan A. Lemme at her Washington Memorial Library and those libraries of Taylor Country – the Reynolds Community Library and the Butler Library. Yet another opportunity for me to register my unparalleled debt to the wonderful lady librarians of the world.

Oregon with that Norfolk in Douglas County – yet another marked only by a post office, serving the inner regions and what was to have been called Norfork due to the junction of two rivers but wisely designated as Norfolk by the main post office. A thanks to librarian Deborah Lipman of the Douglas County library system.

Were youth on my side, what wonderful travels and meetings I could have had – maybe another will take up that mission?

Colorado and Larimer County – no Norfolk remains save a large railway watering tank for those ancient water guzzlers – an outpost on this long railway line. Next door however is the fascinating story of one Charles Buylger who had the vision to lay out a new town with roads and building sites. Only no one ever came. At most it was only a loading site for cattle and sheep. Understandably Charles became depressed and finally was imprisoned for life having killed a man in a gun battle.

Jamaica with its chancy communication channels and its remarkable background history has still a Norfolk and a Norwich community to be identified. The heartening congratulations on progress so far from Central Librarian Theresa Smith led me to the significant Norwich and Norwich Halt, written up elsewhere. Again, my debt to librarians, but Jamaica has to be visited for research on the ground.

The story will continue with yet more lost Norfolks and Norwiches to come to light. They all deserve to be recorded as a history of human endeavour, hard graft, but even within these, lots of laughs, as shown by just such stories from my friends – Clare Tarr of North Norfolk and the charming Dobbin ladies of South Norfolk, Manitoba, Canada.

One of the continuing puzzles is the answer to the question "Why no Norwich and only three Norfolks in that great land mass Australia, where so many of our own peoples went, albeit under unhappy circumstances, in those early days?"

The First World Family Gathering Norwich City, England 1996

THEY ALL CAME!
that is those that we knew of at that time!

THE first world gathering of Norfolk and Norwich communities was engendered in 1996 to coincide with the Lord Mayor of Norwich's annual street parade.

His Worship the Lord Mayor, Councillor Rory Quinn, seen here presenting the scroll of honour, gave leave for us to have some 19 of these communities join the parade by invitation of the many floats that took part.

In addition, our "family'" visitors celebrated with us the 900th anniversary of our Cathedral with the generous co-operation of Dean Stephen Platten, attended a reception by Norwich County Council and we "took over" our equally aged castle for a final farewell with an audience of 600 to include ancient Knights, Cromwellians, our own Morris dancers, and the British Legion entertaining their Canadian comrades.

13

All this supported by both the Norwich Society (Mrs Sheila Kefford) and the Friends of Norwich Museums (Mrs Rosemary Salt), and again with particular honour by the presence of our Lord Lieutenant of Norfolk County, Sir Timothy Colman, at every one of the main events.

Sheringham seamen leading in the 50 lb turkey from Bernard Matthews at the Castle.

The special service at our then 900 year old Cathedral was another of the most memorable highlights.

The Rural Dean congratulating me and my mentor Stanley Taylor in the Cathedral cloisters.

The Bishop of Norwich and Norfolk welcoming "the Family", and astonished that this historical event had come about. The Dean of Norwich Cathedral is to the right.

To me, one of the most heartwarming aspects was the way in which our own citizens extended a welcome by offering accommodation, Sunday lunches and so many more generosities.

Again amongst the many wonders was the reception given by the Royal British Legion to the delegation from the Norwich village, Ontario detachment of the Royal Canadian Legion. A trooping of the Colours and a band concert.

Right: Henry Revell receiving a presentation from Lance Body, Commander of the Ontario detachment. Henry organised that most evocative final to the grand gathering at Norwich Castle, a bugler to sound the "Last Post".

Some of the hundreds of presentations received during those round the world visitations. Do you recognise your own?

THE FIRST WORLD NORWICH & NORFOLK GATHERING

13th to 15th JULY, 1996

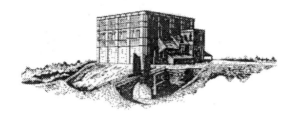

The first reunion since those 17th Century 'Emigrations'

THE CELEBRATION OF NORWICH CATHEDRAL'S 900th YEAR

NORWICH CITY'S 800 YEAR CHARTER

THE 900 YEARS OF NORWICH CASTLE'S FOUNDATION

NORFOLK A COUNTY OF THE
PILGRIM FATHERS AND THE' MAYFLOWER'

NORWICH & NORFOLK
FOR THE FIRST TIME ATTRACTIVELY ON INTERNET

**THE FIRST WORLD
NORFOLK & NORWICH REUNION**

TOWARDS THE THIRD MILLENNIUM

Derek Bickford-Smith, Organiser and Co-ordinator
12 Chapelfield North, Norwich, Norfolk, NR2 1NY. Telephone and Fax: 0 (UK) 1603 614967
E-mail: Norwich.Norfolk@netcom.co.uk. web page: WWW.Gurney.co.uk

THE FIRST WORLD NORWICH & NORFOLK GATHERING
13th to 15th July, 1996
The first reunion since those 17th C entury 'Emigrations'

PROGRAMME—Saturday, 13th July to Monday, 15th July

SATURDAY, 13th JULY
Tour for Norwich & Norfolk visitors. £1 (payment a/c "CEECA").
MORNING, 9.30 a.m. tour of city. **Meet West Door Cathedral.**
An introduction by Norwich Blue Badge Guides.
Coffee and briefing St. Andrew's Church.
Lunch at Norwich Union offices, Surrey Street, 12.00 noon Shopping, etc.
EVENING, 5 p.m. THE LORD MAYOR'S STREET PROCESSION.
Theme: Around the World with Norwich & Norfolk.
All visitors join in the parade with their own area tourist "handouts".
Evening fireworks view from City Hall steps.

SUNDAY, 14th JULY
MID-MORNING:
NORWICH CATHEDRAL THANKSGIVING SERVICE.
Arrive 10 a.m. for 10.30 a.m. service and welcome.
Meet the people in The Cathedral Cloisters.

Royal British Legion (Norwich)
COMMEMORATIVE SERVICE FOR ROYAL CANADIAN LEGION
(Norwich, Ontario)

*The Norfolk & Norwich Peoples' Evening.
U.S.A., Canada, Australia, New Zealand, Norfolk Isle.
Promoting world Norfolk & Norwich, plus leaflets, Choirs,
Medieval Knights, Morris Dancing.
*Visiting World Norfolk & Norwich arrive 6 p.m. for Special Supper,
guided tour Castle/Dungeons. Charge £10 each (Payment A/C "CEECA").
*UK public arrive, 8 p.m. Entry only by prepaid ticket.
£3 each pre-payment A/C "WINC July 1996" per Societies or Organiser.
Battlement/Dungeon Tours. Visit Exchanges. Crafts, Barber Shop and
Sea Shanty men choirs. Morris Dancers,
Medieval and Cromwellian Knights.
*In co-operation The Administrators of The Friends of Norwich Museums,
Norwich Society, Norfolk Society.

MONDAY, 15th JULY. Norwich & Norfolk 'Visitors' only.
10 a.m.   Farewell Reception for Visitors at Norwich City Hall.
12 noon Farewell Reception for Visitors at Norfolk County Hall.

SUNDAY, 14th JULY
Norwich Society/Friends of Norwich Museums

NORWICH CASTLE GRAND RECEPTION

900 years old . . .intimate past connections with some ancestors?

OBJECTIVE:

To enjoy meeting . . . make friends . . . exchange addresses . . .

understand each others communities

ENSURE A FUTURE COMMITMENT!

8 p.m. Castle and Museum open to our Norwich and Norfolk People.
Our visitors will be coming at 6 p.m. for Morris Dancers, private tours and "al fresco" supper.
Norwich Castle and Museum guides will offer tours.

8.15 p.m. Norwich Museum Rotunda.
The Sea Shanty Men of Sheringham will process . . .
"The Norfolk Turkey", donated by Mr. Bernard Matthews, C.B.E.
THE BLESSING OF THIS
FIRST WORLD NORFOLK & NORWICH GATHERING.
The Norwich Barber Shop Choir will welcome.
Tours of Battlements and Dungeons (time permitting).
Guides available to the many interests of the Castle Museum.
Visit/Travel Stands . . . focal points for each community.
U.S.A., CANADA, AUSTRALIA, NORFOLK ISLAND, NEW ZEALAND.
LOCAL CRAFTS, MEDIEVAL KNIGHTS, CROMWELLIAN PURITANS.
CASTLE SHOP AND BAR

8.50 p.m.
Choirs will give alternate presentations in The Castle Keep and Rotunda.

EVERYONE IN THE ROTUNDA
9.45 p.m.
THE CHOIRS WILL JOIN TOGETHER IN THE ROTUNDA leading the singing of "AULD LANG SYNE".

Master of Ceremonies: THE BOB BRISTER.

18

The Second World Family Gathering Norfolk Island, South Pacific 2000

In the year 2000, we held the second international gathering of "the Family" on Norfolk Island, that very much alive dot in the South Pacific near Northern Australia and New Zealand.

The originator was Alan Kerr and organisers Fred and Nan Smith.

Above: with the ultimate organiser – Angela Guymer
Right: another central figure, Gillian Reckitt
(between another bloom – my wife, Huguette, and a thorn – me!)

The present Administrator, the Honorable Tony Messner (centre), retired Administrator, the Honorable Alan Kerr (right), and on the left – guess who?

Which one would you buy a secondhand car from???
But seriously, before I too am "exported" to Norfolk Island to mirror those hard times of old....

There again was the evidence of this new found totally inclusive friendship.

We were welcomed by the Island Administrator. Attended a celebration of the anniversary of Captain Cook's landing (Captain Cook was there himself). Visited the annual Norfolk Island's Agricultural Show – the one and only, outside our own country.

There was a Church of England celebration service with their wonderful community hymn singing that made the rafters jump up and down, let alone ring, and a planting of a commemoration tree on which we receive an annual "well-being" report.

Above, some of the "Family" members at the 2000 gathering.
Look at those smiling faces!

Agnes Hain who originated this unique facility also organised that we plant a tree in memory of our visit. Pictured with me is Tim Christian (related to that original mutineer on the Bounty).

Probably one of the most endearing aspects of the Gathering was the traditional "Norfolk island hug" as so efficiently practiced by ex Australian Norfolk Island Administrator, Alan Kerr. It has to be given and felt to be really appreciated. Quite the best of gestures for world peace.

EVERY DAY IS A "HUG" DAY!

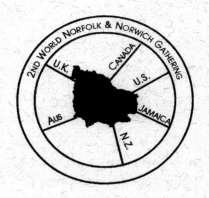

AN ORDER OF EVENING SERVICE

for
The 2nd World Norfolk and
Norwich Gathering

at
All Saint's Church of England
Kingston, Norfolk Island

on
Sunday, 8th October 2000.

PROGRAMME

National Anthem - God Save The Queen

Welcome - Rev. Ian Hadfield

Hymn 350 - All People That On Earth Do Dwell

Order of Evening Service
(Page 17 - Book of Common Prayer)
Led by Dr. John Duke

Bible Reading - Matthew 9:1-13
Mr Derek Bickford Smith

Choir Item - "Celebration of Praise"

Bible Reading - Colossians 1:15-23
Mr Alan Kerr A.M.

Norfolk Anthem
Words and Music by Alan Kerr A.M.
Arrangement by Eric Craig MBE.

Norfolk Island home to me
With stately pine and deep blue sea
In as much I'll join with thee
And honour Norfolk Island
Honour Norfolk Island

Norfolk's peaceful Norfolk's free
Safe and sure 'twill always be
In as much we'll speak for thee
And honour Norfolk Island
Honour Norfolk Island.

God protect and keep us blest
In our toil and in our rest
In as much let's give our best
And honour Norfolk Island
Honour Norfolk Island

Apostle's Creed - page 22

Prayers and Collects - pages 25, 42, 43, 26

Interview
Wayne Marshall - Bible Society

Hymn 547 - The Lord's My Shepherd (Crimond)

Sermon
Reverend Ian Hadfield

Offertory Hymn 377 - O For A Thousand Tongues to Sing

Prayer of Thanks

Benediction

Vesper

Sing-a-long - Led by Tom Lloyd A.M.

Choir Mistress Julie South - *Organist* Tim Lloyd A.M.

Future
"Family Gatherings"

The 2006 Gathering in Canada

A splendid prospect of Canadian autumn in Norfolk County, Ontario, Canada, at the County Agricultural Fair.

We shall be (officially) 10 years old! People to people and schools to schools, organisations to organisations, Canadian/British Legions, friendship groups, Lions, Rotary, Round Table, Masons, Churches, Museums, the Women's Institute (they began here!), all meeting their opposite numbers as guests.

The 2008 Gathering in Tasmania

New Norfolk, Tasmania
Jacky Whitehead and Damian Bester (editor Valley Gazette) organising.

Check www.netcom.co.uk/norfolk/ for the latest news

England
United Kingdom

The English Flag

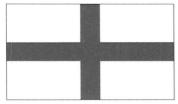

The cross of St George, patron saint of England since the 1270s, is a red cross on a white ground. It was the national flag of England until James I succeeded to the throne in 1603, after which it was combined in 1606 with the crosses of St Andrew and St Patrick to become the "Union Jack" – the national flag of the United Kingdom.

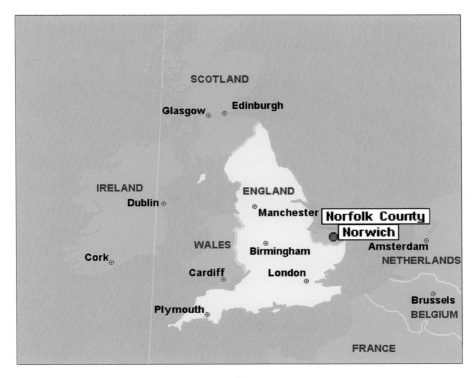

The Early Emigrations
by Ian Smith

Why Norfolk?

"The prospect of transatlantic emigration for such people would have been akin to a voyage to the moon for us. Indeed it was even more daunting than a space shot." Such was one of the conclusions reached by Roger Thompson in his exhaustive study of East Anglian participation in the Great Migration to New England.

What then motivated these seventeenth century emigrants and others who came after to launch themselves into the unknown? And are there any special factors which apply in particular to those Norfolk men and women who abandoned their native county?

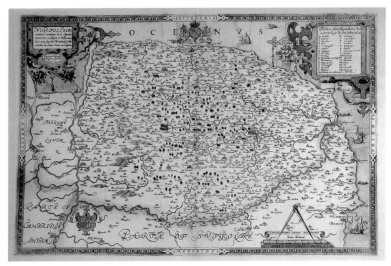

Map of seventeenth century Norfolk

One such factor was a spirit of commercial enterprise, thanks to which Norwich had already developed into a thriving, outward-looking city and Norfolk into the centre of a successful textile industry.

Among those Norfolk adventurers seeking fresh fields to conquer were a handful who helped to establish the very first English New World settlement in Virginia in the early 1600s.

Without outstanding individuals such as John Rolfe of Heacham this fragile foothold may not have survived at all. He saved its economy by introducing tobacco, its first commercial crop, and ensured at least a temporary truce with its native inhabitants by his marriage to their Chief's daughter Pocahontas.

Portrait of Pocahontas on the Heacham village sign

Another factor driving early emigration from Norfolk can be traced to a long tradition of non-conformity and dissent dating right back to the Peasants' Revolt, Kett's Rebellion and the Lollards. Some 20 years after the Virginia settlement several thousand Norfolk Puritans, inheritors of this non-conformist tradition, left their native shore in the footsteps of the "Pilgrim Fathers" to establish a pure "Bible Commonwealth" in Massachusetts Bay away from the increasingly intolerant religious climate in England.

Part of a predominantly East Anglian exodus – which became known as the Great Migration – their contribution to the New World was less in terms of outstanding individuals, and more in terms of collective ideals. According to one commentator the way of thinking later characterised by Franklin Roosevelt as the Four Freedoms "appeared in Massachusetts within a few years of its founding". The libertarian ideas of the early colonists were "deeply embedded in Puritan ideas and also in East Anglian realities".

After these initial migrations Norfolk genes continued to play a crucial role in the subsequent political history of the North American colonies and later of the U.S.A.

Thomas Paine, the Thetford-born political radical, did more than anyone to change the course of the dispute with the mother country from protest to rebellion and then to independence.

Statue of Thomas Paine in Thetford, Norfolk

Abraham Lincoln, directly descended from an apprentice weaver who emigrated from Hingham via Norwich in 1637, was perhaps the greatest of all American Presidents.

Emigration is the subject of the Hingham sign

Later migration from Norfolk – both to North America and elsewhere – was generated more by "push" than "pull" factors. A rising rural population combined with an agricultural depression, for example, drove 3,354 people from Norfolk villages to Canada between 1835 and 1837, helped and encouraged both by their unions and the parish ratepayers. Others were going even more involuntarily – on the convict ships to Australia. But whether their migration was voluntary or not, these Norfolk men and women of humble origin all helped to populate and develop these two great dominions.

Place names are then only one aspect of the imprint of Norfolk in distant lands. From commercial adventurers and Puritans to impoverished farmers and convicts, all Norfolk migrants made an important and distinctive contribution to their adopted countries.

Norfolk Textiles
by Helen Hoyte
Vice President of the
Costume & Textile Association for Norfolk Museums

Before recorded history and throughout the centuries, Norfolk was famous for the quality of its wool and cloth. The wealth the industry brought built 657 gothic churches; today they stand in silent testimony to the merchant adventurers who traded far and wide, and built churches in the hope of escaping some hideous medieaval purgatory.

Norfolk's natural advantages of flat pasture land, with numerous inland waterways, suited sheep farming and with many ports around the coast, easy access allowed the export of wool and cloth all over Europe.

hot combers   fulling   bleaching   Carding

Spinning   weaver   Searching cloth   cloth sealing   tailors shop

For centuries huge quantities of Norfolk wool were sold abroad. Early records show that the highest poundage of wool exported came from Norfolk.

In the middle of the fourteenth century, Edward III forbade its export; he ordered that Norfolk wool must be kept for cloth-making and immigrant cloth-workers from Flanders, with new techniques, were brought in to boost the local industry. In mediaeval times Norwich was a Staple City; here powerful Guilds, intent on maintaining a reputation for high quality cloth production, set the standards. All woven goods were examined and could not be sold unless they had been passed, carrying the Norwich stamp to prove it.

Worstead, a tiny village in North Norfolk, gave its name to the world famous cloth still known today as worsted. Despite wars, plagues and famines the industry prospered until the early sixteenth century when fine worsted and woollen cloths went out of favour.

In 1556 cloth workers (known as the Strangers) were brought to Norwich from Holland and Flanders to revive the failing industry. They introduced a variety of luxury cloths called the "new draperies" and "outlandish commodities", different fabrics made with mixtures of silks, wools, linens and cottons. After the restoration of the monarchy these colourful, varied and reasonably priced cloths, now became known as the "Norwich Stuffs" and were highly fashionable, bringing great prosperity to the city and county throughout the seventeenth century.

During the eighteenth century Norwich merchants or their agents travelled all over Europe with comprehensive pattern books, selling a variety of cloths including brocades and damasks, particularly in Russia where "Norwich stuffs" were greatly favoured at the court of Catherine the Great.

As the industrial revolution took hold, the bulk of cloth-making moved to the North of England; the old cottage industry gave way to the factory system and Norfolk, without access to cheap coal, lost its place in textile manufacture. However, production of high quality fabrics survived, with Norwich manufacturers continuing to use hand-loom weaving. During the eighteenth century expensive shawls were coming to Europe from Kashmir. European manufacturers tried to copy them and Norwich manufacturers, using a traditional cloth that had the softness and lightness of cashmere, pioneered the manufacture of shawls and were well placed to met the huge demand which developed. Competition between the European centres of shawl production was keen, throughout the nineteenth century. By producing beautiful, high quality, well designed, long and square shawls, woven of silk and worsted, pure silk and some mixtures of yarns, the Norwich industry catered for and successfully appealed to the fashionable elite of Victorian society.

1844 Norwich Turnover Shawl 3.22 m x 1.52 m. Silk warp: wool weft with wool and some silk fill over. Manufactured by Towler & Campin. This striking colour was known as "Norwich red".

Norfolk County
England
United Kingdom

Population: 800,000.
Administration: Elected Council of 60 members.
Area: 2,050 square miles.

Norfolk, England – the parent of all the world namesakes, where our story really begins....

The county is thought of by many as being flat because there are no hills of any consequence, but minor hills and valleys abound in a gently rolling landscape. There are, of course, areas that are completely flat. In the west, below the Wash, is a vast area known as the Fens. Countless dykes and ditches dug over the centuries have now drained the land. And in the east, the rivers now meander through the remains of once vast estuaries that lead to the sea. Around the coastline the landscape is continually changing as the soft cliffs are eroded by wind and tide. Countless houses and even whole villages and towns have disappeared beneath the waves over the centuries. So Norfolk is a county of contrasting landscapes from the fens in the west, across the downs of the north, the wetlands in the east, and the heathland of the south. And everywhere, towns and villages with over a thousand years of history.

Norfolk and its neighbour, Suffolk (the lands of the North Folk and South Folk), form the original East Anglia – land of the Angles – and before the Angles, the land of Boudicca and the Iceni. An area steeped in history.

By the time the Normans invaded in 1066, Norfolk was one of the most populated counties in England – for the Domesday Book, Norfolk required two books! It was a prosperous farming county, and it has remained such.

Farming methods of times past are still remembered at a number of country shows around the county in the summer months.

Norfolk County Council welcomes "the Family"

Presentation of our "Family Plaque" (on wall behind) to Norfolk County and the County Chairman Councillor Dr James Norris.

And then a reception for the New Norfolk delegation from Tasmania to ensure that we would agree to a world gathering there in 2008! Headed by Damian Bester, Editor in Chief of the New Norfolk Gazette. Seen here signing the visitors book with John Shepherd.

A reception by Norfolk County Chairman Councillor Colleen Walker for the recently retired Australian Administrator of Norfolk Island, South Pacific, Alan Kerr (left) and Gillian Reckitt (right). The latter's ancestors include the original "Christian" of Mutiny on the Bounty fame.

Alan Kerr "holding forth" at the reception joined by the Lord Lieutenant of Norfolk County, Sir Timothy Colman (right).
Note the Norfolk Island flag and the "World Family of Norfolk and Norwich" map on display.

The Norfolk Coat of Arms

The top part of the shield shows a lion from the Royal Arms of England together with ostrich plumes and coronet referring to the Prince of Wales. This is a very special honour for the county. The use of the design was granted in commemoration of the Royal Family's association with Norfolk: they have a residence at Sandringham.

The lower part of the shield comprises the arms attributed to Ralph de Gael, first Earl of Norfolk c. 1069. The ermine may well refer to Brittany, as Ralph was Lord of Gael in that Duchy.

The lion represents the City of Norwich, and the lion joined with a herring the Borough of Great Yarmouth. Both were former county boroughs and were re-absorbed into the county in 1974.

The County Council provides the strategic and more costly services like social services, education, museums, libraries, police and roads. There are seven Norfolk districts, each with its own elected council providing the more local services. Some district councils are called borough or city councils. And there are hundreds of "parish councils" that look after the needs of the individual villages.

King's Lynn and West Norfolk

King's Lynn is the largest town in the West Norfolk area, a port with a long history associated with the sea. George Vancouver was born here in 1757. Later, as a captain, his voyages took him to Canada where he founded the town that now bears his name.

A somewhat tenuous link with America is that location shots for the 1985 Al Pacino film "Revolution" were filmed in King's Lynn with the Custom House (seen above) pretending to be in Philadelphia!

Farther up the coast is a real connection with America: the village of Heacham, where John Rolfe brought his bride Pocahontas.
Heacham is also the home of Norfolk Lavender.
Not far away is Sandringham, the Norfolk home of Her Majesty The Queen, where the Royal Family spends Christmas.

Another stately home in the area is Holkham Hall, home of the Earl and Countess of Leicester. The Coke family built the hall, and the fifth generation Thomas Coke did much to influence farming methods in the early nineteenth century.

The beach at Holkham made a brief appearance at the end of the film "Shakespeare in Love" as the desert island Gwyneth Paltrow walks ashore on.

Around the coast are many villages and small towns with creeks that offer great sailing providing you keep an eye on the tides!

Not too far inland is Burnham Thorpe, the birthplace of England's most celebrated sailor – Admiral Lord Nelson.

Wells-next-the-Sea is probably one of the best kept secrets of Norfolk. It has a wonderful mix of "quayside" activity, holiday bustle and Georgian houses whilst maintaining a peaceful countryside feel.
Despite being over a mile from the open water, Wells is one of the few Norfolk towns which has maintained a commercial port.

At Castle Rising are these remains of a Norman stronghold modelled after Norwich Castle. Here Queen Isabella, the "She-Wolf of France", was kept after she was caught plotting the murder of her husband, King Edward II.

North Norfolk

Cromer is widely known as "the gem of the Norfolk coast". Strange to think, looking at this view from the cliffs, that centuries ago Cromer was a mile or so inland with the coastal village of Shipden out there beyond the end of the pier.

By the end of the eighteenth century Cromer had become a fashionable place, no doubt helped along by one of Jane Austen's characters in "Emma" referring to it as "the best of all sea-bathing places". The opening of railway lines from Norwich and the Midlands in the 1890s marked a great expansion of the town with the grand hotels and houses that still dominate the sea views. By 1900 the esplanade and the pier completed the "look" of the town we see today.

Cromer still retains its link with the sea. The boats lined up at the bottom of the Gangway still bring home "Cromer crabs", considered the best crabs you can get; and on the Gangway itself the former lifeboat station is now the RNLI Henry Blogg Museum, with displays on the life on Henry Blogg and the other brave lifeboat men that risked their lives to save others, and the restored lifeboat H. F. Bailey.

And around Cromer, the villages of East and West Runton, Mundesley all have their small fleets of crab boats.

Characteristic of the area are the cottages faced with the smooth flints collected off the seashore.

And at Sheringham, the old railway station is now headquarters of the North Norfolk Railway. They offer a 10.5 mile round trip by steam train (vintage diesel trains on some journeys) through this delightful area of North Norfolk.

Inland now, and this is Blickling Hall, near Aylsham. Today a Jacobean house; in earlier times the Boleyn family had a manor house here. Henry VIII's Anne Boleyn may have lived here.

Broadland

In the eastern half of the county, Broadland is unique. Over 200 miles of navigable waterways with no locks. Several rivers slowly wind their way towards Great Yarmouth and the sea, and along many of them are more than 30 'broads' – lakes of all shapes and sizes – attached to the rivers. They were thought to be natural until the mid-twentieth century when research revealed that they are in actual fact the flooded results of peat digging in the twelfth to fourteenth centuries when peat was used as domestic fuel. The other natural product of the area was (and still is) the reeds and sedge used for thatching.

The coming of the railways at the end of the nineteenth century opened up this then "unknown" area to holidaymakers and an

industry based around water holidays was born.

Today cruisers, dinghies and yachts of all shapes and sizes provide a more relaxed style of holiday where the speed limit is 5 miles per hour!

Along the river sides, charming villages and pubs that today provide for the tourists – both land and water based.

In times gone by, "wherries" – wide flat-bottomed boats – were the workhorse of the broads, carrying goods across the county. Today, a few have survived and have been converted to pleasure craft.

Amongst the larger boats that provide pleasure day trips is a small replica of a paddle-steamer that would probably be more at home in the U.S.A.

Great Yarmouth

The view above from the ruins of the Roman Fort at Burgh Castle looks across the marshes and reclaimed land that was in Roman times a 6 mile wide estuary at the coast. In those days a sandbank was starting to form at the mouth of the estuary. Over the centuries the sandbank grew and was first settled by fishermen attracted by the abundant herring in the North Sea, then traders and shopkeepers moved in, and slowly a town was born.

In 1849 Charles Dickens visited Great Yarmouth, and the story of David Copperfield was born. The south part of town today is filled with the industrial estate and the Pleasure Beach, but in Dickens' day it was just sand-dunes, and there could well have been an old fisherman living in a converted upturned boat there....

The herring brought prosperity to the town. For centuries, the vast fleets of fishing boats stayed at Yarmouth during their travels down the coast following the shoals of fish. Scottish girls followed the fleet to gut and process the fish, which they did with lightning speed that amazed everyone who saw them. And they never wore gloves to protect their hands from those very sharp knives or the ice!

Around the town were many "smoke houses" where the herring were smoked to produce the famous Yarmouth kippers.
Sadly, the sea was overfished, and the industry has now gone....

Today, much of the quayside activity revolves around being a supply port for the oil and gas platforms in the North Sea....

... but during the Maritime Festival, the supply ships have to share the quay with vessels from other times.

Great Yarmouth is Norfolk's premier seaside holiday resort.
Yarmouth's beach – a mile of the best sandy beaches in the area – is called "the Golden Mile".

And of course, there are all the usual features of a holiday resort – the rides on the Pleasure Beach fun fair, arcades, shows, and the gift shops of Regent Road, which luckily has been pedestrianised.

South Norfolk

Just south of Norwich,
the town of Wymondham
(pronounced Windham) has
retained its character thanks
to a by-pass of the busy A11
road which used to wind
through the town.
Today, even the by-pass has
been by-passed!

In the centre of town, the Market Cross is a well known landmark.
Today it houses the Tourist Centre – the best in the county.

Wymondham Abbey has a
unique feature – the result of
a long dispute between the
Abbey and the townspeople
over the use of the church. In
the end the townspeople built
their own tower at the other
end!

The tower was later the scene of the sad end of William Kett, brother
of Robert Kett, who led a rebellion against the Enclosure Act in 1549
which allowed the landowners to fence in the common lands where
the ordinary citizens used to graze their cattle. Kett rallied an army
that besieged and for a short while held Norwich as a protest on
behalf of the common people. It took an army of over 10,000 to get
the city back. The Ketts were eventually captured, tried, and found
guilty of treason. Robert was hanged at Norwich Castle. William
suffered the same fate on the tower of Wymondham Abbey.

Today, Hingham has the look of a Georgian town but it is in fact much older. Here in 1622 Samuel Lincoln was born. Samuel became apprenticed to Francis Lawes, a weaver in Norwich. On 8th April 1637, when he was 15, he sailed with Lawes and his family in the "John and Dorothy" of Ipswich for America, eventually settling in Hingham, Massachusetts. Samuel's great-great-great-great-grandson was Abraham Lincoln, who became the sixteenth President of the U.S.A. Members of the Lincoln family in the United States erected a bronze bust memorial in St Andrews church in 1919.

Down on the Norfolk/Suffolk border the town of Diss sits on a hill around an ancient lake called the Mere.
A few miles away is the village of Bressingham, home of the Bressingham Steam Museum and Gardens.

Breckland

In the very centre of Norfolk
lies the town of East Dereham
with a unique town sign that
spans the High Street.
It illustrates the story of St
Withburga, daughter of the
Anglo-Saxon King Anna, who

founded a convent here in the seventh century. Legend has it that at
a time of famine some does from the local herd of deer made their
way to Withburga every day so they could be milked. After her death,
pilgrims journeyed to her tomb.

Three hundred years later the Abbot of Ely seized her remains and
took them back to his own cathedral. A spring which was claimed to
have curative properties sprang from the empty tomb. Withburga was
proclaimed a saint and even more pilgrims flocked to the town.

The spring can still be seen
in the church graveyard
which also has a memorial
gravestone for a French
prisoner of war shot trying
to escape from the bell tower
during the Napoleonic wars.

Today, Dereham is typical of the
market towns in Norfolk. The weekly
market brings traders from across the
county, and attracts locals and visitors
alike.

The Breckland area is full of towns with legends.
In Swaffham lived John Chapman, a pedlar, who went to London and met a stranger who told him of a dream in which he found a fortune buried in an orchard in some place called Swaffham. The pedlar rushed home, and digging in his orchard found a pot of gold.
And just outside the town of Watton is Wayland Wood where the legend of the "Babes in the Wood" comes from.

Near the Norfolk/Suffolk border is the town of Thetford whose market town appearance hides its importance in Saxon times. Thomas Paine, author of "The Rights of Man", was born here.
It was also the home of Charles Burrell & Sons,

whose steam engines were world famous.

The southern part of Breckland is primarily heathland, large areas of which are taken up by USAF air bases and the British Army weapons ranges. Thetford Forest is today mainly pine trees planted by the Forestry Commission.

Norwich City
Norfolk County, England
United Kingdom

Population: 121,000.
Administration: Lord Mayor and 39 Councillors.
Location: 52°37'26"N 1°17'36"E.

The 1,000 year old "parent" to the world Norwich communities.

Today a city of great contrasts, with medieval streets like Elm Hill and modern buildings like the Forum.

The city centre within the city walls (which encompass an area larger than any other city in England) still retains the layout of roads which date back to the times when the many Saxon settlements started merging together to become Norwich.

The early Norwich had a turbulent history. The Vikings raided the town many times, and eventually eastern England surrendered to the Danish King Sweyn in 1013. Many of the streets in Norwich have names of Danish origin.

When the Normans arrived in 1066, Norwich was one of the largest towns in the country. From the Domesday Book we know that when they built the castle and its earthworks they demolished at least 90 houses and several churches.
The castle still dominates the city centre today.

Tombland (which means "open space") was the Anglo-Saxon market place before the Normans arrived. Based on an ancient crossroads, it is believed that the palace of the Earls of East Anglia stood at the

southern end.

At the northern end of Tombland, the Maid's Head Hotel with its Georgian "mock Tudor" appearance stands on the site of a much earlier inn.
Charles Dickens stayed here.

Augustine Steward's House, now home to a collection of antique dealers, was built in 1530. Today a tranquil scene, but the building looked upon some of the bloodiest fighting during Kett's Rebellion in 1549.

The Cathedral and its precincts stand to the east of Tombland. The building was started in 1096 and took nearly 200 years to complete. The stone used was shipped from Caen in Normandy.

After the townsfolk set fire to the cathedral in the riots of 1272, the timber roofs were replaced with stone vaulting with carved and painted roof bosses – the first use of story bosses anywhere. There are over 1,000 throughout the Cathedral and cloisters, now being carefully restored.

In 2003 Norwich celebrated 600 years of Mayoralty with pomp and ceremony at St Andrews Hall...

Today the Lord Mayor uses modern transport for most of his travels, but on all too rare occasions he uses the Lord Mayor's Coach.

St James's Mill (built 1839) stands as a monument to the failed attempted to revive the declining wool trade which had moved to the industrial north of the country.

The weaving trade was the first of Norwich's industries to disappear.

The shoe industry, which was built up from dozens of small businesses and eventually saw massive factories built, has now gone, with Start-rite, the last of the shoe factories, closing as production is moved to the Far East.

Norwich once had two pubs for every day of the year, and many large breweries to keep them supplied! The breweries, like most of the pubs, have now gone.
So too have the great engineering works of Boulton & Paul which produced aircraft during the Second World War. And Lawrence Scott Electromotors, which made some of the world's largest electric motors.

Today, the largest employer in Norwich is the Norwich Union

Insurance Group, its original grand building now swamped by the company's ever growing office blocks that now cover a large area of the city. As for the future, who knows? Norwich Union has just started using call centres in India. How long before they too leave the city....

The city centre is traditionally based around the Market Place – the largest open air market in England, open six days a week. It has stood on this spot since Norman times.

Beneath its multicoloured canvas roofs an "Aladdin's cave" of goods and services is available.

Besides the fruit and vegetables, meat and fish stalls, there are clothing, tools, electronics, books, records, and even an internet cafe. The Market Place is due for a modern "make-over" in 2005.

Overlooking the market are the old and new seats of local government – the Guildhall (on the right) and City Hall.

The Guildhall is a large complex building, reflecting the status of Norwich at the time of building (1410) when the city was amongst the largest and wealthiest cities in England.
Its many rooms include council chambers as well as justice courts with the accompanying prison cells.

The current City Hall was built in 1938, though never completed due to the Second World War and a subsequent lack of funds. At the northern (clock tower) end you can still see the stub girders on the unfinished section.

HMS Norfolk
United Kingdom

Norfolk County, with its 100 miles of coastline, has always had a strong connection with the sea, from the brave fishermen who help feed us, to one of our greatest National heroes – Nelson, who learned to sail as a child near his birthplace in Burnham Thorpe, Norfolk.
So it is fitting that the Royal Navy should mark that connection with a ship named Norfolk.

The current HMS Norfolk was built at Yarrow Shipbuilders Ltd on the

Clyde and launched by Her Royal Highness Princess Margaret, the Countess of Snowdon, on the 11th July 1987 and accepted into Naval Service on the 24th November 1989. She is the sixth ship to carry the name and is the first in the 'Duke' class of frigates.

She has a complement of 177 (not including Flight).

A detachment from HMS Norfolk joined us for the first ever gathering of the World Norfolk and Norwich Communities in 1996 in Norwich, England.

In 1988 HMS Norfolk received the freedom of the City of Norwich. During his visit I met Commander Williamson of HMS Norfolk to invite the crew to the Second World Gathering on Norfolk Island. Unfortunately, duties prevented their joining us. We hope for better luck with the 2004 Gathering.

Previous HMS Norfolks

The first HMS Norfolk (1693–1749) was an 80 gun, third rate ship of the line. Built at Southampton, the ship displaced 1,184 tons and was later rebuilt in Plymouth after earning her first battle honour at Velez Malaga.

The second HMS Norfolk (1757–74) was a 74 gun third rate. Built at Deptford.

The third HMS Norfolk (1807–12) was a cutter hired for naval use.

The fourth HMS Norfolk (1927–49), a County Class cruiser of 9,925 tons displacement was laid down on the Clyde 8 July 1927, and launched 12 December 1928. She distinguished herself during the Second World War, playing a significant role in the actions that resulted in the sinking of the German Bismarck and Scharnhorst. Her battle honours include Atlantic 1941, Arctic 1941–43, North Africa 1942, North Cape 1943 and Norway 1945.

The Fifth HMS Norfolk (1967–82) was launched by Lavinia, Duchess of Norfolk in November 1967.

Norfolk   Norwich

Connecticut State U.S.A.

The Connecticut State Flag

On a field of azure blue is an ornamental white shield with three grapevines, each bearing three bunches of purple grapes. The State's motto "He who Transplanted Sustains Us" is displayed on a white ribbon. The vines stand for the first settlements of English people who began to move from Massachusetts in the 1630s. These settlements were thought of as grapevines that had been transplanted.

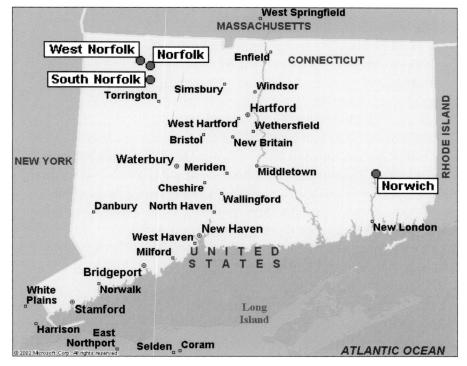

59

Norwich City
New London County
Connecticut State, U.S.A.

Administration: City Council.
Population: 38,000.
Location: 41°31'27"N 72°4'35"W.

Norwich City Hall

Norwich, Connecticut, is the best known of
all the world Norwich communities outside
England. It is situated on the River Thames, thus
continuing the many connections with England
and the remarkable number of similarities
with its namesake city in the English county of
Norfolk. As well as a well defined river (with
a power source so sadly lacking in Norwich, England), it had an
original wool trade etc., even to its own impressive City Hall!

Today, Norwich has lost much of her manufacturing capacity. Vast
mill buildings still line the River Thames, but they are converted
for other uses. One of the last industries was the making of vacuum
flasks. Another was the city historian, Dale Plummer's try to revive
that extensive woollen manufacture of past years, but it all became
too difficult to obtain the right raw materials.
Norwich is nationally known for its unique mixture of architectural
styles including Federal, English Colonial, Colonial Revival, Queen
Anne, Italianate, Greek Revival, Victorian Gothic, Tudor Gothic,
Roman Classic, Richardson Romanesque and Art Deco – to name but
a few. The focal point for all this is the totally renovated City Hall, a
solid example of French Second Empire architecture.

Norwich CT's houses of worship range from the austere white-clapboard first Congregational Church of the United States of America – twinned with the original Congregational Church of Norwich, England – to the majestic spire of St Patrick's Roman Catholic Cathedral.

There are many wonders that Norwich houses within its 10 council districts; however, if one be worthy of mention it is the magnificent museum of the Norwich Free Academy – the Slater Museum. A magnificent display, second only to the British Museum in its collection of copies of the sculptures of Europe's many civilisations.

Left: the Slater Museum

The first visit to Norwich, CT

My first visit to any Norwich or Norfolk community outside the UK was in 1993, a commencement to contacting "discovered" communities in New England and a taste of the welcomes received in so many more on that twice round the world marathon over the next three years and the delivery of some 60 talks on my home Norwich and Norfolk communities.

Dale Plummer, city historian, was delegated to be my guide, and arranged a remarkable couple of days with opportunities for meetings, radio broadcasts (my downfall on radio was on being asked "How's the family?" I replied that I had not had time as I had only been there a few hours), and press coverage, plus meeting the people – from an octogenarian lady, who was difficult

Happy memories of the stay in the Armstrong Home on my first visit in 1993

to find until we discovered her tilling her garden as "the young couldn't be trusted to do a thorough job!" – to the workers in Dale's own start-up wool weaving mill, mirroring those days of that trade and utilising one of the remaining vast buildings built for that purpose along the riverside. Of the "public" meetings so excellently arranged, the primary question was always "Where is Norwich and where is Norfolk in England?" – a question that is to be repeated at all the communities I have visited – much to the disbelief of my own fellow citizens who have that factor "of being the most important" at least in common with all their namesake communities!

Dale Plummer, who acted as my guide during that first vist to Norwich

The extrememly powerful and popular delegation from Norwich, at the first ever Family Gathering in Norwich, England in 1996!
In the background a statue of Admiral Lord Nelson, a Norfolk man.

The second visit to Norwich, CT

There was a second visit, this time with citizens from Norwich, England in 1999. Here again, we all stayed with private households and visited the City Hall, church and school – a wonderful experience that would benefit everyone from both communities!
It is time we had them back!

Norwich Connecticut City Hall 1999. Presentation of the World Norfolk and Norwich Communities plaque to Norwich City by the delegation visiting in 1999. You will recognise Peg Tumicki (left), our organiser for that wonderful "meeting the people"! and Doris Ball (holding the plaque).

Some of us found the Norwich Police very attractive!

The Lafayette Memorial with Margaret Tumicki, our best of best organisers. Without the French, American Independence would have been much harder.

And weren't those welcoming hostesses absolutely charming!

Norwich, Connecticut history

Native Americans were the inhabitants the English explorers had to deal with, and as far as Connecticut was concerned, in 1637 a force of 90 Englishmen and 70 natives from the friendly tribe of Mohegans made their way down the Connecticut River.
Their aim was to attack the original inhabitants and as yet unfriendly Pequot tribe. This they did with a throughness that almost exterminated the Pequot. Thus the Mohegans occupied the land bordering the Thames River and in their subsequent war with yet another tribe whose demise is recorded in the history of Norwich as

"the Indian Leap" – a ravine down which the remnants of this tribe were forced to leap to their death.

The fine grazing lands and sparkling streams persuaded a large proportion of the neighbouring town of Saybrook to remove and make a settlement called Norwich.

Thus, with 69 founding families, Norwich began as an accomplished community rather than a gradual evolvement in 1659.

By 1694 there was a public landing area at the head of the Thames River, and Norwich Town was serviced by two main roads which became Washington Street and Broadway.

The Carpenter's shop. One of the late eighteenth century buildings in the old Norwich Town area.

In the first instance goods were shipped direct from England, but the Stamp Act of the English Parliament in 1764, which put a tax on all such goods, forced Norwich to become more self-sufficient. Factories and large mills developed with the water power afforded from the fast moving rivers. Woollen mills, timber processing and later on armaments were thriving industries.

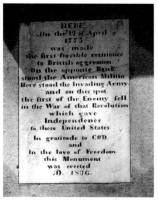

It is a matter of history that such taxes became the basis for American independence, and battles were fought against the English, with Norwich becoming the leadership centre.

Two fateful battles decided the course of the American Revolution in 1777. These resulted in the English forces aided by contingents of German and Canadian militia being overcome, and the French throwing in their power behind the American forces.

Norwich's individual history concerns, amongst many others, a remarkably "fiery" Norwich-born gentleman, General Benedict Arnold, whose courage and leadership contributed greatly to these victories. However despite his injuries which made him no longer a fighting soldier, he finally lost faith in his fellow generals whose intentions were to diminish his achievements, and he went over to the British. History in Norwich has branded him as a traitor, but it may be that this has gradually been less emphasised in view of his exemplary achievements for American independence. Arnold is buried in England, whilst Norwich has many memories of all nations in its Old Burial Grounds.

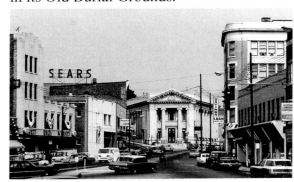

Left: downtown Norwich in the 1970s

Part of an "aero-view" drawing of Norwich in 1912

New London County, Connecticut – from an 1895 Atlas
showing Norwich – both City and Town, which are now merged into one

All too little about wonderful Norwich CT – the oldest and the
largest of the Norwich communities in the United States of America.
Save to relate one experience during the four meetings I addressed
while there.... At one meeting, one of the audience rose to his feet
to declare "We are no longer a colony, we are independent!" I found
it difficult to reply adequately until his third interruption when I
declared in my turn, "But now we are friends!"
There was a remarkable cheer from the audience.
Another event that comes to mind was my being presented with a
silver token from the enormous centre for gambling in the nearby
Native American Reservation. Maybe one day a million dollars???

Norfolk Town
Litchfield County
Connecticut State, U.S.A.

Administration: Board of Selectmen.
Population: 1,700.
plus some seasonal 4,000 more.
Location: 41°59'38"N 73°12'9"W.

The Town Green

The Congregational
Church of Christ

Norfolk is home to three bed and breakfasts and two inns, and
with two state parks within its boundaries Norfolk is a well-loved
destination for travellers. The "downtown" has, amongst all the
necessary shops, a pub with 250 types of beer! and a remarkable
connection with Norfolk UK through an antique dealer called Joseph
Stannard – a namesake of a member of the famous first regional
English school of painters based in Norwich, Norfolk, UK! Is
he related? He was invited to visit our Norwich UK and it would
certainly cause a great deal of interest in artistic circles.
I wonder if he really believed me?

A history of Norfolk CT

Norfolk CT about 1850

Norfolk was named in May 1738, and incorporated in 1758 with
44 voters at the first town meeting. A meeting house was built and
in 1761 the Reverend Ammi R. Robbins became the first minister,
serving for 52 years.

Twenty-four men from Norfolk marched to aid Boston in 1775 and
over 150 fought in the Revolutionary War.

The early settlers were farmers, erecting sawmills, gristmills,
and smithies for their own needs. Using the waterpower of the
Blackberry River, the town became industrial in the 1800s,
manufacturing such diverse products as linseed oil, men's hats,
woollens, cheese boxes, scythes, and hoes. In the later nineteenth
century, industry declined, but the coming of the Connecticut
Western Railroad in 1871, together with Norfolk CT's natural beauty,
contributed to the growth of a thriving summer colony.

Norfolk has been a center of culture since the establishment of the
Norfolk Library in 1888 and the Litchfield County Choral Union
in 1889. The famous Music Shed on the Stoeckel Estate, often
visited by many of the world's greatest musical artists, is now the
home of the Yale Summer School of Music and Art.

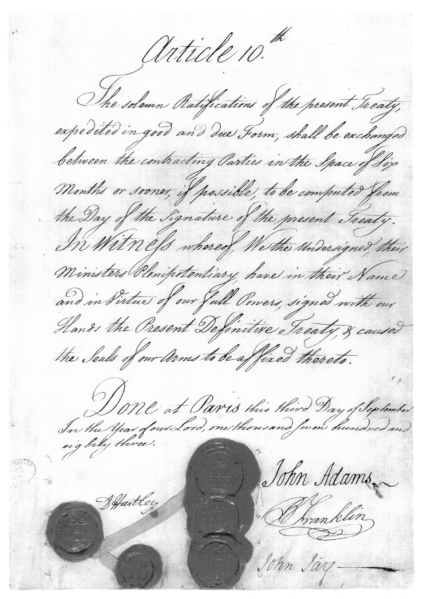

Article 10.th

The solemn Ratifications of the present Treaty, expedited in good and due Form, shall be exchanged between the contracting Parties in the Space of Six Months or sooner, if possible, to be computed from the Day of the Signature of the present Treaty. In Witnefs whereof, We the Undersigned their Ministers Plenipotentiary, have in their Name and in Virtue of our Full Powers, signed with our Hands the Present Definitive Treaty, & caused the Seals of our Arms to be affixed thereto.

Done at Paris this third Day of September In the Year of our Lord, one thousand seven hundred and eighty three.

D Hartley

John Adams.

Franklin

John Jay

Copy of the peace treaty of 1783 formulated in London and signed in Paris
by John Adams and Benjamin Franklin,
and "found" by Derek 2002 in London, England

70

The first visit to Norfolk CT

My first visit to Norfolk in 1993 began with the being welcomed by Louise Schimmel, the Library Director. And that evening after attending a church choir practice, being regaled by songs whilst giving vent to the only one I could remember – namely "Do ye ken John Peel?" and allowing myself to give full vent to the "View Hullo"!

The night I stayed with those delightful people Debbie and Colin Tait in their "wonder house" (no locking of doors!).
They came to that first ever Norfolk and Norwich World Gathering in 1996.

The Taits with the Norwich City Crier representing Norfolk CT at the first ever Family Gathering in 1996

Thence to a morning's tour led by historian and museum curator Gay Fields (and my first experience of an "American" sandwich!).
Then an afternoon drive around by Louise to the settlement of self contained Huddite people's houses. (Was it there I was shown a staircase with the middle steps three time higher so as to make marauding Indians stumble? Visiting seven communities in 14 days makes the memory confused.)

This was followed by an evening arranged for me to give a talk on my own country. How fortunate for historical records that the tape machine was found not to be working!

More about Norfolk CT

The Norfolk Library is located on the Village Green in a magnificent red sandstone building designed by Hartford architect George Keller

Library interior

and built in 1888.

It has regular exhibitions and most remarkably, to a visitor from Norfolk England, the complete collection of the numerous tomes of Blomfield's History of Norfolk England – something that is rare even in its country of origin.

Norfolk children attend the elementary school in town and then go to the regional high school in Winstead.

Of the three churches the Congregational church used to have a mandatory attendance of its citizens; very much in line with the medieval law of England. Now there is also a full time Roman Catholic church with an Episcopalian church just for the summer time.

Tales of Times Past

Dentistry in 1822 was only concerned with extraction and the story is told of a doctor on his rounds meeting a man with toothache. They were both on horseback and the doctor reined close in, grabbed the tooth with his "turnscrew" and applied his spurs to gallop off with the tooth! It is said that no charge was made for the operation!

(Credit: North Norwich NY)

The second visit to Norfolk CT

The second visit was in 1999 when we had a delegation from Norwich and Norfolk County UK. How enormously impressive and enjoyable that was for everyone in their different "home stays'" and a "bean feast" or rather Italian rice feast organised by Louise's own Louis!

Louis, Head Chef and his "bottle washers"

AND THEIR CAKE!

It was during this visit we presented a copy of the World Norfolk and Norwich plaque to Louise, for display in her library, as representing the hosts Norfolk Town CT.

John Rosenblatt, first selectman presenting the 1999 delegation with Norfolk Town's emblem

Left: Desmond Elias from Norwich England, making the most of his birthday celebration with the attractions of Norfolk CT

West Norfolk, Litchfield County, Connecticut
Location: 42°0'11"N 73°13'29"W.
West Norfolk is about 2 miles north-west of Norfolk Town.
South Norfolk, Litchfield County, Connecticut
Location: 41°55'23"N 73°12'28"W.
South Norfolk is about 6 miles south of Norfolk Town.

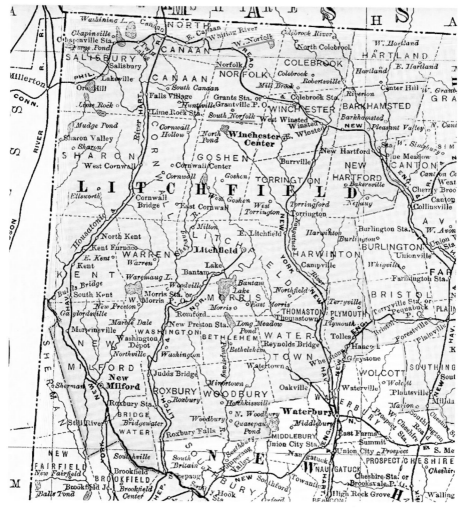

Litchfield County, Connecticut – from an 1895 Atlas

WORLD FAMILY
www.gurney.co.uk/norfolk

Norfolk Norwich

North Dakota State, U.S.A.

The North Dakota State Flag

A dark blue field displays a bald eagle holding an olive branch and a bundle of arrows in its claws. In its beak, the eagle carries a ribbon with the words "One nation made up of many states". The shield on its breast has 13 stars, representing the original 13 states. The fan-shaped design above the eagle represents the birth of a new nation, the United States. The name "North Dakota" appears on a red scroll below the eagle.

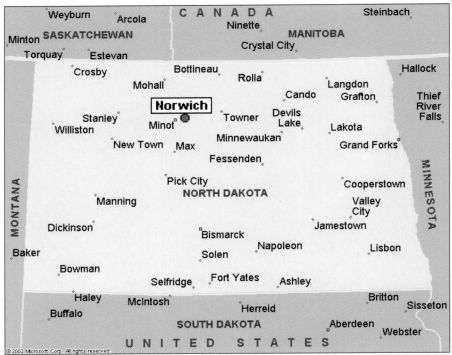

76

Norwich
Minot, McHenry County
North Dakota State, U.S.A.

Population: 50?
Administration: Mayor and 6 Councillors in Minot.
Location: 48°14'47"N 100°59'19"W.

Norwich Lutheran Church

Norwich ND history

As generously given by Ruby Mogard via her daughter Juell Brababant.
Ruby has been the Lutheran Church organist for over 45 years!

Plot of land filed in 1901 by Eugene W. Stubbins and named
Norwich, possibly after a railroad surveyor as the English were very
involved in railway construction and Norwich was a thriving railroad
centre. In those days Norwich had everything except a "saloon"
and still has none with its current church and large grain elevator
– this latter grain elevator is in line with the predominant agricultural
interests of North Dakota – although there are oil and coal resources.
Norwich is also associated with the largest earth-filled dam in the
world – Garrison Dam Lake Sakakawea.

My visit in 1995

As I crossed over the border from Manitoba, Canada, I called in on the Peace Garden and this in April weather that was sleeting, with the "roads" some 5 inches of mud over a still frozen base.
My car was that sandy sludge colour all over!
The gardens looked like they could be attractive were the weather

The International Peace Garden.

in better form. A totally open international boundary and all traffic passing freely between Canada and the United States of America on the 49th parallel. The International Peace Garden is a 2,339 acre botanical garden commemorating peace between the United States and Canada along the world's longest unfortified border. It blooms with more than 150,000 flowers and showcases the Peace Chapel.

Finally, I arrived in Norwich.
Right: Mrs Klein at the Post Office, who had my previous messages pinned on the information board but showed a Norwich distrust of strangers, especially one so untidy in a mud-stained car having driven all the way from the Manitoba Norfolks! Friendly, but no "cup of tea" on that dismal morning. Thus a 1,000 mile journey for a mere 10 minute meeting.

Why was it that whenever I asked for the directions to North Dakota, the inevitable reply was "nobody ever GOES to North Dakota!", when in all my discoveries I found that NORTH DAKOTA IS THE GEOGRAPHICAL CENTRE OF NORTH AMERICA! and Derek was there!

McHenry County, North Dakota – from an 1895 Atlas

Dakota

Author Unknown

When skies of the north beam a fathomless blue,
And mirroring lakes rival heaven's own hue,
When banks of sweet roses and cherry in bloom
Are ravishing sense with their tints and perfume,
When challenging bobolink vie with the lark
In rollocking rondos from daylight 'til dark,
I murmur a prayer as in rapture I stand
"God bless thee Dakota, my beautiful land."
And then when I see what the people have wrought,
The farmsteads, the cities, the fight they have fought,
A wilderness conquered by brawn and by brain,
A paradise fashioned from valley and plain,
The thousands of homes with their beauty and grace,
The hope of the nation, the flow'r of the race,
Then pride swells my heart and my voice leads the cheer –
"Hurrah! for the sturdy, the brave pioneer!"

Contributed by Mary Lindbo, 2001

WORLD FAMILY
www.gurney.co.uk/norfolk

Norfolk   Norwich

Iowa State, U.S.A.

The Iowa State Flag

Having three vertical stripes blue, white and red, the Iowa flag resembles the flag of France. On the white stripe is a bald eagle carrying a blue streamer in its beak. The state motto "Our Liberties We Prize, and Our Rights We Will Maintain" is written on the streamer. The name of the state is emblazoned in red letters.

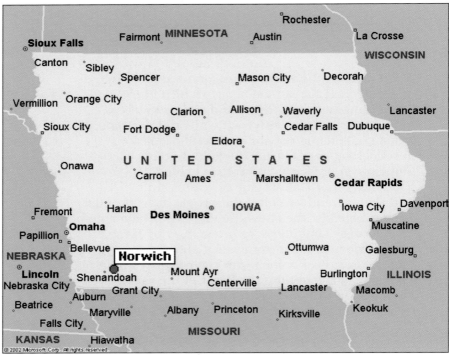

80

Norwich
Shenandoah, Page County
Iowa State, U.S.A.

Population: ?
Location: 40°44'33"N 95°15'23"W.

We have to thank David Crisp, originally from Norwich, England, and now citizen of the U.S.A. for the discovery of this settlement. (Photographs by David)

My visit to Iowa

My visit to Iowa in 1994 found me in the town
of Shenandoah. Memories linger from my
school days of the song with the line,
"Oh Shenandoah, I love your daughter,
but away I'm bound to go, 'cross the wide
Missouri."
Well, now I've found you !

Right: the High School Bell Shenandoah

The humble pumpkin.

Can it ever be really
meant for this?

SCARY!!!

"Six houses and a church", I was told in Shenandoah, "what do you
want with that?" "It is a Norwich living community," I replied, "and
is as important as any other in this world family!"

The town of Norwich was platted (laid out) in November 1882. It
was a station on the Humeston & Shenandoah Railway.
The first store was opened at the end of 1882 along with a post office.
A second store followed in 1888.

Over the years Norwich has had its fair share of fires. The Methodist
Church has burned to the ground twice. The Presbyterian Church,
which was founded in 1882, burned at the turn of the last century and
was never replaced.

Iowa has another two Norwich communities – in Jones County and Wright County. Not found – yet, but we shall succeed!
How do I know? Sharyll Ferrall, now in Alaska, told me! And how did she become interested? She was at school not very far away! And is now at the other end of the world with her son Jason!

We have found a vague reference to a Norwich Cemetery near Anamosa in Jones County, but that's as far as we've got.

Can I appeal to the United Methodist Church or anyone in Norwich, Page County and the Norwich communities in Jones County and Wright County to contact me. We'd love to hear from you.

Kansas State, U.S.A.

The Kansas State Flag

On a navy blue field is a sunflower, the State flower. Also, the State Seal and the words "Kansas". In the picture of the State Seal are 34 stars representing the order of statehood. Above the stars is the motto "To the Stars Through Difficulties". On the seal a sunrise overshadows a farmer plowing a field near his log cabin, a steamboat, a wagon train heading west and Native Americans hunting bison.

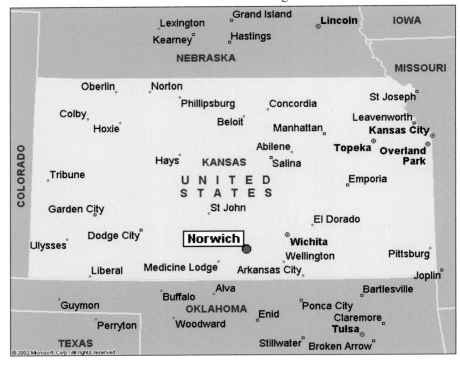

Norwich City
Kingman County
Kansas State, U.S.A.

Administration: Mayor and Council.
Population: 500.
Location: 37°27'26"N 97°50'55"W.

At its peak, Norwich had about 1,500 persons. Today it's a
progressive town of about 500 people, also filling the needs of
surrounding farm families. The four churches in town are Baptist,
Christian, Church of Christ, and United Methodist. There are new
modern spacious grade and high schools in use.
Friendship meals are served five days a
week at the Recreation Center.

Friendship meals

The Farrar Corporation was founded
in the 1930s by E. C. Farrar. They
currently employ 80 persons to produce
ductile iron castings for equipment
manufacturers throughout the United States.
Doug Eshnaur purchased the grocery store in 1983 and is currently
operating it. Harry Eshnaur started Eshnaur Hardware in 1946.
In 1979, Gary and Deanna Vavra purchased it and are currently
operating it. Additional businesses include a bank, appliance and
general merchandise store, honey shop, barber shop, beauty salon,
two restaurants, a truck stop, grain elevator, jewelry store, repair shop
book store, and car lot. There's also a City Hall, post office, library,
Lodge hall, a solar house (Methodist parsonage) and Wheatland
Manor, a senior citizen complex.

My visit to Norwich Kansas

My travels took me there in 1994. There was never a more pleasant welcome that that at Kansas Airport by Jim Skillen, Karlene Skillen and Richard Ross.

Jim and Karlene had taken me on "unseen" and have been the stalwarts of our contacts ever since. Richard, (an aircraft designer who had previously been to England) is sporting his Norwich City UK badge given him by my originator of this world research, Stanley Taylor.

What followed was an intensive couple of days which took in visits to all aspects of Norwich and a talk.

This photograph is blurred but gives an idea of the whole joy of my visit – the joke was about the Norwich Union fire mark. Without the fire mark the fire would not be tackled by the Norwich Union fire men – they would merely watch it burn!

But even more amusing was the question "Was it worthwhile insuring anyway?" as the firemen were entitled to the house contents for their work!

The Honourable Mayor and Mayoress ldon Schragg (of 23 years standing!). I was fortunate to be there in his last year. A busy man – he was also Fire Chief!

Right: Here is a remarkable character I met during my visit.
His background is that he was taken in the Second World War from being a farmer's boy to becoming the pilot of a vast "flying fortress" aeroplane ... and then back to farming in his homeland of Kansas!

What was that we were drinking? No, not whisky, but refreshing iced tea! Reminds me of the school prize giving where on entering the hall to see these beakers all lined up ... a steaming hot evening ... I thought "how sophisticated these schools are ... glasses of beer!" It was quite a shock to find that it was cold tea, but quite understandable and none the less welcome.

Parliament at 9 a.m.!

The morning "parliament" at Eshnaur Hardware – (with Deanna's coffee and treacle cake!) was the most agreeable community meeting place where common subjects were brought up in friendly discussion.

This excellent community experience was repeated in most of the medium to small sized Norfolks and Norwiches worldwide!

A lesson that could well be repeated elsewhere?

The Old Norwich Fire Bell

This bell was purchased by Norwich in 1912 for use as a fire bell. It was used until it was replaced by an electric siren in 1939. This monument was erected in 1985 by the Norwich Jaycees in honor of Norwich's progress in the first 100 years.

Plaque donated by Farrar Corporation

A history of Norwich
Kindly provided by Karlene Skillen, historian

The City of Norwich was in the Osage Indian Trust lands. The townsite was purchased by William Willhower and James Skillen. The surrounding farms and ranches in this "wheat state" and the arrival of the railroad made it an excellent site for a town.
Amongst the sophistications there was even an Opera House and within some of the many new inhabitants was a colourful character called Everitt who was an excellent carpenter except when the town "druggists" sold him too much "joy juice".
Doctor Eugene Wallace moved in 1928 and immediately established a ten-bed hospital.
Norwich was confirmed as a third class city and E. N. Haag was elected first Mayor.

Karlene and Jim Skillen came to that very first gathering of the Norwich and Norfolk Family in 1996 ...

In the Lord Mayor's parade they were transported in a wagon that could well have been of the same breed as that of her pioneer ancestors – and cheered by the 20,000 strong crowds that learned, probably for the first time, of Norwich, Kingman County, Kansas, U.S.A.

Massachusetts State
U.S.A.

The Massachusetts State Flag

A blue shield with the image of a Native American, Massachuset. His arrow is pointing downward representing peace. The white star represents Massachusetts as one of the original 13 states. Around the shield is a blue ribbon with the motto: " By the Sword We Seek Peace, but Peace Only Under Liberty". Above the shield is a arm and sword, representing the first part of the motto.

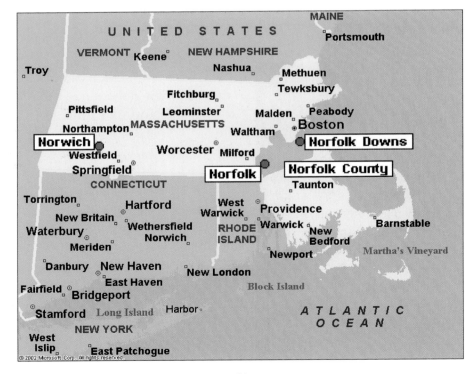

Norfolk County
Massachusetts State
U.S.A.

Population: 620,000.
Land area: 400 square miles.

Excerpts from the History of Norfolk County
by Dorothy Peck, County Administrator

In 1793, Dedham was selected as the shiretown for the new County
of Norfolk MA, and an influx of lawyers, politicians, and people on
county business forced the town to abandon its traditional insularity
and its habitual distrust of newcomers.
(This is a real "Norfolk" touch – all Norfolk people are traditionally
distrustful of newcomers!)
The county of Norfolk MA, as first incorporated, included all the
original territory of Suffolk, except for towns of Boston and Chelsea.
On May 10, 1643, the Colony of Massachusetts Bay was divided into
four counties; Essex, Middlesex, Suffolk and Norfolk. Thus Norfolk
County originally had the towns of Haverhill, Salisbury, Hampton,
Exeter, Dover and Portsmouth.
Salisbury, Hampton, Exeter and Dover were set off to New
Hampshire with state separation in 1680. The remaining towns were
set back to Essex County on 4 February 1680 and the original County
of Norfolk ceased to exist.
Norfolk County MA consists of 28 eastern Massachusetts
communities, located to the south and west of Boston. The County
was incorporated as a regional governmental entity in 1793, and has
its county seat at the town of Dedham.

(There are a remarkable number of communities that have an history and name that relate to England and indeed a significant portion of the original population came from our own Norfolk County ,England.)

Norfolk County MA is proud of its heritage. It is the only county in the nation to boast of having four Presidents – John Adams, John Quincy Adams, John F. Kennedy, and George Herbert Walker Bush. The Adams National Historical Park is situated in the City of Quincy and the family story is that of five generations (1720–1927) to include two Presidents and First Ladies, three United States Ministers, historians, writers and family members who supported these public figures.

Norfolk County MA has 185 farms and on average their size is 53 acres and they employ 42 workers who are on the farm more than 150 days per year. The major crop is greenhouse and nursery production whilst the second is vegetables and the third dairy.

Our visit in 1993

Exchange of presents between Walpole Massachusetts and Lord Walpole of Norfolk, England. Ella Carstairs of the English delegation (right).

Presentation of the World Norfolk and Norwich Founder Member Plaque.
Henry Ainslie (left – my first stalwart correspondent with English connections and retired County Administrator), Major Anthony Gurney (centre) presenting one of our plaques to William O'Donnell, Chairman of Norfolk County (right).

Visit to the Norfolk County Agricultural School in Walpole MA.

Future agriculturalists with Major Anthony Gurney (left), and College Principal Richard C. Morse (right)

Some fun with history in Boston, Massachusetts ...
the English helping get rid of that troublesome tea!

The Norfolk County
Massachusetts
plaque presentation
to Councillor Roy
Durrant, His Worship
the Lord Mayor of
Norwich City, in the
Lord Mayor's parlour
back home in the UK.

Footnote: You are now looking at writings of the Hon. Deputy Sheriff
of Norfolk County Massachusetts, as appointed by the High Sheriff,
Clifford H Marshall!
I should try telling that to a policeman who catches me speeding!
Derek

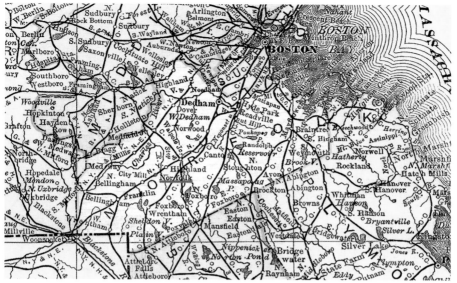

Norfolk County, Massachusetts, from an 1895 Atlas
showing the location of Norfolk Town

Tales of Times Past

Amon Merrit was justice of the peace in the days when
justice was often settled out of court.... One day a man
noted for creating trouble and notably unreliable was in
an hotel and involved in an argument with a young man
whom he challenged to conclude the disagreement outside.
This was accepted and very soon the challenger was getting
the worse of the conflict and called out "Enough Enough!"
He was about to be relieved of the beating he was receiving
when Amon Merrit, who was standing by, said, "You had
better hit him again, Reuben, he always lies and you have
trouble in telling whether he is telling the truth."

Credit to North Norwich "Galena"

Norfolk Town
Norfolk County
Massachusetts State, U.S.A.

Population: 10,500 (and growing).
Administration: Board of Selectmen.
Location: 42°7'10"N 71°19'32"W.

The town is governed through a
Board of Selectmen, each elected for
a three-year term, and is administered
on a day-to-day basis by a Town
Administrator who is a town employee.

The magnificent Town Hall

Norfolk history
With the guidance of Mrs Thelma Ravinski and Betsy Pine
(both of the Historical Commission)

Although first settled in 1669, Norfolk was not incorporated as a
town until 1870, when it broke away from Wrentham and other
surrounding communities. The area formerly known as "North
Wrentham" has gone through many changes over the years.
The reason for naming it Norfolk? Unknown save for the possibility
that it was originally the north part of Wrentham and thus "North
folk"? The partition took place in 1869.
Norfolk has a radio station and a cable station for local news whilst
there are organisations including the Lions, the Grange, Garden Club
and Norfolk Community League. Three churches (one Catholic) and
three schools. Every year in June a Community Day is celebrated
around the bandstand.

96

Norfolk schools

The Norfolk Public Schools include the new H. Olive Day School on Main Street, for students from pre-kindergarten through second grade, and the Freeman/Centennial School on Boardman Street, from grades 3 through 6.

After sixth grade, Norfolk students join students from Plainville and Wrentham in the King Philip Regional School District. Grades 7 and 8 attend includes the King Philip North Middle School in Norfolk, while grades 9 through 12 attend the King Philip Regional High School located in the adjacent town of Wrentham, Massachusetts.

Other schools in the area include the Tri-County Vocational High School in Franklin and the Norfolk County Agricultural High School in Walpole.

Local preschools include the Norfolk Elementary School's integrated preschool and two private preschools – the Norfolk Cooperative Preschool and the Norfolk Children's School.

NB:- The King Philip referred to above would be Metacomet, the Wampanoag tribe son of Massasoit. The King Philip war fought in this area was a devastating one.
Thanks to John Spinney, Norfolk Public Library for that information. (It was not the King Philip of Spain as I had first suggested!)

TROOP 80 – Norfolk Scouts

Norfolk Cub Scouts Pack 125 is for boys in grades 1 to 5 who live north of Main Street. Many special events are held throughout the year such as the rocket launch, the pinewood derby, and the blue and gold banquet. Cubmaster: John Hurley. Another potential for international contact?

More historical notes
by Geri Tasker who teaches in nearby Medfield and Thelma Ravinski
of Norfolk Historical Commission
(Geri has visited her sister parish, Metfield, England)

Settlers, with the agreement of the local Indians, used the lands
that had been cleared for grazing their animals, and in 1675 after a
disastrous war led by the Indian Sachem King Philip there grew up
the area of Wrentham. The railroad later serviced the area.
Fires have been the great destroyer of first housing and thus the
importance in every community of the fire stations. The new Town
Hall was completed in 1998.

My visit in 1993

Norfolk Town is another of these remarkable communities of
America and that short taste given me in 1993 ... the church service
with a christening ... the presentation of the town insignia ... and a
remarkable meeting with a blind chorister who demonstrated how
gardening was excellently managed for such a disability by having
a string map as guidelines! ... and even more remarkably having just
retired from being the chief cook at the local school for many years!

Yet another potential disaster during the visit was the sudden loss
of my hearing, in that my battery went flat in the middle of the
presentation by the Senior Selectman. I had to interrupt and say that
I couldn't hear, and that my spare battery was in the car two blocks
away! All this was taken with great calm – my presenter took me
there in his car and we returned to take up where we had left off!

Next door at Foxborough, and its Boyden Library, the Chief
Librarian was Bertha Chandler. Bertha had been the American

Librarian at that unique Library in Norwich UK – the largest American Library in England. And what a wonderful job she did in those few years with the schools and associations of Norfolk County, England. It was wonderful to meet her again!

A Norfolk Town rug was presented in 1993 to a delegation from Norfolk, England. Now with Norfolk Museums Service, England – a fabulous gift!

Centre: Geoff Woodrow, Senior Selectman Norfolk Town
Right: William P. O'Donnell, Chairman Norfolk County Commissioners

In 2003, Norwich, England was honoured with a visit from Jacqueline and Dr John McFeeley, Chairman of the Norfolk Town Selectmen, Massachusetts.
This photograph shows us being welcomed to Norwich Castle by a seventeenth century Sheriff of Norwich.

Norfolk Downs
Quincy, Norfolk County
Massachusetts State, U.S.A.

Norfolk Downs is a suburb of Quincy.
Location: 42°16'20"N 71°1'15"W.

After finding a mention of 'Norfolk Downs' in Massachusetts on
the internet, we finally made contact with the Thomas Crane Public
Library in Quincy. Our thanks to Mary Clark at the library for
providing the following information in newspaper cuttings...

Right: Extract from the
"Patriot Ledger" newspaper
dated Nov. 30th 1928

CAUGHT OFF THE AIR

I understand that the special re-
searchers of the Thomas Crane public library were thrown into turmoil
this week by a telephone query as
to when and how the section of this
city known as Norfolk Downs got
its name. Search of local histories
and casual reference to old newspapers failed to bring the slightest
record of the matter, though when
Librarian Hill mentioned the matter
to Planning Chairman Wilson Marsh
the p. c. recalled that there was a
prize offered for the name.

Strange to think, here we are 75 years later, asking the same question!
And now we can tell you the story of Norfolk Downs....

100

In 1890 the town of Quincy, south of Boston was expanding. The firm of Wood, Harmon and Co. had started developing the old Indian lands north of Quincy. Wollaston Park was the first real estate project in 1890. By 1892 they were ready to expand north, and as a way of advertising the new development offered a prize of a house lot for whoever came up with a suitable name for the new project.

Older residents in the area wanted it to be called "Massachusetts Fields" – its old name from colonial times – but the developers wanted a new name.
Miss Louise Murdock, a schoolteacher, suggested "Norfolk Downs" in rememberance of the low hills of the old country. The name was accepted and she was presented with the deeds for the $1,000 lot.

Sketch of Norfolk Downs Railway Station
from the Quincy Daily Ledger, April 16th 1892

Norwich
Hampshire County
Massachusetts State, U.S.A.

Population: ?
Administration: ?
Location: 42°7'10"N 71°19'32"W.

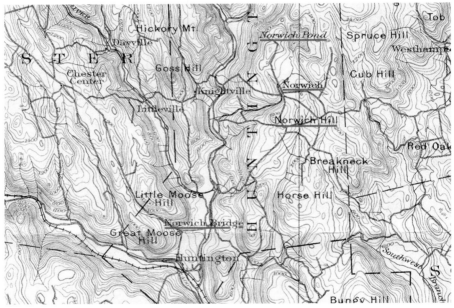

Another unexplored area. This 1895 map shows a Norwich, a
Norwich Bridge, a Norwich Hill, and even a Norwich Pond! that
still appear on present day maps. Internet searches have only so far
provided limited and confusing information, mainly because of there
being a Huntington Town and Township, and it's not certain which
the following is referring to …

Huntington was created from the eastern part of Murrayfield and named "Norwich". It was renamed Huntingdon in 1855. Two major divisions within the town were "Chester Village", near the railroad station, and "Chester factories", later the incorporated town of Chester.

The First Congregational Church was gathered as Norwich First Church in July 1778, at Chester Village ("Falley's Crossroads"). The First Parish was organised in 1832. The church was renamed when the town's name was changed. The church was incorporated in 1917, and called itself "the Church on Norwich Hill."

(To add to the confusion, the nearest Chester we could find is Chester Town in Hampton County, over 7 miles to the west!)

Michigan State U.S.A.

The Michigan State Flag

A deep blue field has three mottoes: "One Nation Made Up of Many States", "I will Defend" and "If You Seek a Pleasant Peninsula, Look Around". On the shield the sun rises over a lake and peninsula, a man with raised hand and holding a gun represents peace and the ability to defend his rights. The elk and moose are symbols of Michigan, while the eagle represents the United States. Flag adopted 1911.

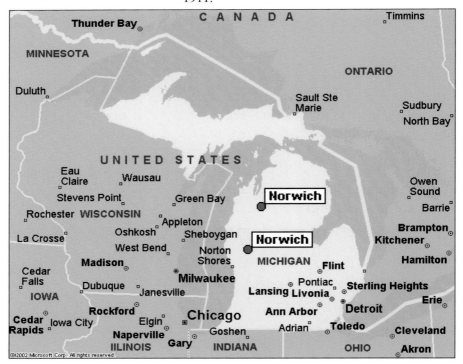

104

Norwich Township
Missaukee County
Michigan State, U.S.A.

Administration: Supervisor, Clerk, Treasurer and two Trustees.
(The township hall is in Moorestown.)
Population: 650.
Area: 72 square miles.

Norwich Township is located in the northwestern corner of
Missaukee County. The county was named after a prominent Indian
Chief, Nesaukee, which means: "Large Mouth of the River".

This remote township is one of the few remaining double-sized
townships in Michigan, spanning 6 by 12 miles. The eastern half is
located in the Missaukee State Forest and contains several streams
and creeks that form the Dead Stream Swamp. Oil also has been
found here, and many wells dot the landscape.

The small community of Moorestown is known for having an airport
and is a popular place in the summer months for fly-ins with those
who have small aircraft.

We have the pleasure of three writings from pupils at Lake City High School, Missaukee....

Angie Klein, Lake City High School, 10th grade, 16 years old

"I've lived in Norwich Township my whole life. I live in a safe community. You can trust just about everyone. It's nice because you can walk down the road and wave at someone and know at least their names. You are friends with their kids and your parents are friends with the kids' parents."

Quinn Vokes, Lake City High School, 10th grade, 15 years old

"Sunny day in the Church yard, swinging back and forth, being called in for cookies, greeted by an angel's face and a warm smile. She tells us a simple bible story and we listen intently. Lesson is over. We skip down the dirt road home singing 'Jesus Loves Me.'"

Erin Milne, Lake City High School, 12th grade, 18 years

"To live in Norwich Township is to have a real sense of community. I have had the sort of childhood that is difficult to come by these days. My old friends live within biking distance. I know each one of my neighbors. The saying about it taking a whole village to raise a child is true here. I don't feel I have missed out on anything having grown up in a small town."

And Lois Milne (Clerk and Treasurer of Norwich Township) remarks:
"This is Easter time with spring around the corner. I remember Easter baskets consisting of pickled eggs and one toy and maybe if we were lucky a chocolate. I am attempting to send something of a surprise to my daughter in Italy. It would be her first Easter without the Easter colouring of eggs and hunting for Easter eggs with her basket."

The history of Moorestown by Fred C. Hirzel on the internet is fascinating, and the building of that community from the raw beginnings is there to be understood.
Web site: http://www.rootsweb.com/~mimissau/moorestown.html

We have found reference to a Norwich village in neighboring Pioneer Township, but have no more information as yet.

Tales of Times Past

Squire Bockee owned some 500 acres, and was successfully enterprising. He was a plain man and used to ride around on an old buck board wagon.
One day a man with a fine turnout stopped him and called to him "Squire Bockee, you should be ashamed riding into town on that old wagon!"
"Neighbour", said the Squire, "the man who rides in this wagon can afford to pay his debts!"
Needless to say the critic owed Squire money.

(Credit to North Norwich NY)

Norwich Township
Newaygo County
Michigan State, U.S.A.

Administration: Supervisor, Township Clerk, and two trustees.
Population: 560.
Area: 35 square miles.

Newaygo County was named after Chippewa tribeChief Naw-wa-goo, one of the signers of the Treaty of Saginaw in 1812. Settlement of the area began in 1836 when Michel Charleau took a group of businessmen from Chicago up the Muskegon River and observed the great expanse of white pine there. The first sawmill was built by the Pennoyer brothers a few years later at the junction of the Muskegon River, and a creek bears their name a few miles northeast of what is now the city of Newaygo. The lumber boom in the last half of the 1800s was very good to this area, and put the county on the map. The Muskegon River, Michigan's largest, became the lifeblood of the area, first for transporting lumber, and later for hydroelectric power. Three huge dams were built after the turn of the century: Croton, Hardy and Newaygo. Croton and Hardy Dams remain today, with Hardy the largest earthen dam east of the Mississippi.

Newaygo County today relies on tourism as its main economic support, with agriculture and small manufacturing secondary. The Muskegon River continues to be the main attraction for summer cottage residents and fishermen, who find it nearly the best source for fish – steelhead in the spring and salmon in the fall – anywhere in Michigan. Hunting, camping and RV'ing are also excellent, as over half the county is contained in the Manistee National Forest.

About Norwich Township
Generously supplied by Deb Parrish, Local History Librarian,
White Cloud Community Library

Based on the lumber industry and first instituted in 1872, Norwich
Township's population of 637 in 1880 had doubled by 1884, such
was the growth of the industry.
Today the township poplulation has withdrawn to its earlier figure.
There were five schools but they have now disappeared.

There appears to be no information as to why the name Norwich, but
it is suspected that this comes from members of another Norwich
community that moved here at that time.

The township has five lakes, of which the largest is one of the sources
of the Pere Marquette River. There was a logging railroad and a
post office. By 1926 the railroad has disappeared, yet the post office
remains.

While today there appears to be one church at Woodville, the rest of
the township is greatly divided into small lots, and what remains of
the forest is on the Western Boundary.

We hope for more news of Norwich Township and its tourist
attractions as the internet communication develops.

Woodville Station
about 1900

Minnesota State
U.S.A.

The Minnesota State Flag

The flag is royal blue, with a gold fringe. In the center of the flag is the State Seal. Around the State Seal is a wreath of the state flower, the lady slipper. Three dates are woven into the wreath: 1858, the year Minnesota became a state; 1819, the year Fort Snelling was established; and 1893, the year the official flag was adopted. Nineteen stars ring the wreath. The largest star represents Minnesota.

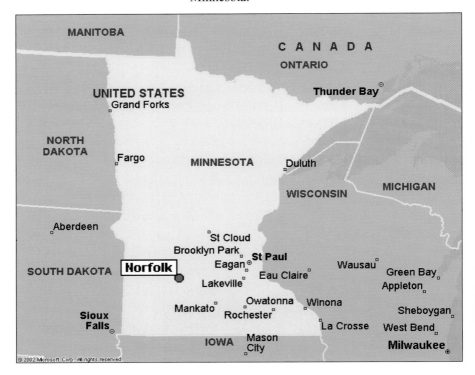

110

Norfolk Township
Renville County
Minnesota State, U.S.A.

Administration: Township officer, three supervisors.
Population: 200.
Area: 35 square miles.

Norfolk is a small country community with a small township house at an intersection, surrounded by fields of which the main output is corn, beans, wheat, sugar beet and cattle.
There is a Rural Beauty shop, a recreational vehicle business (campers) and a seed plant; while children are bussed out of the township for school. Otherwise no church, library or grocery stores. A family-oriented community.

Renville County is an agricultural county located in west central Minnesota. The county is well known for its agricultural innovations including crop and animal cooperatives, seed crop breeding and production and farmers willing to experiment with newly developed agricultural technology.
Renville County was named for Joseph Renville, a famous pioneer in the west central frontier of Minnesota. Renville was born in 1779 in the village of Kaposia. His father was a French fur trader and his mother a Dakotah and member of the Little Crows band of Sioux. Renville at the age of 10 was sent to Canada to study the French language and the fundamentals of the Christian religion under the guidance of a Catholic priest. Upon his return to Minnesota he served as a guide and interpreter for the government and fur trading companies.

He established his own trading post at La Qui Parle where he later died. Renville is remembered as a friend to the Sioux Indians and white travelers alike. His relationship with the Indian tribes was instrumental in maintaining peace for the new frontier.

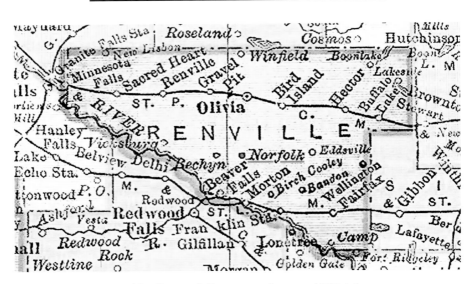

Renville County, Minnesota – from an 1895 Atlas

Nebraska State
U.S.A.

The Nebraska State Flag

The State Flag is national blue with the State Seal in gold in the centre. The picture in the seal shows a train in the background, with mountains in the distance, a steamboat on the Missouri River, a simple cabin and wheat sheaves, and a blacksmith working at his anvil. At the top of the seal a banner holds the motto "Equality Before the Law".

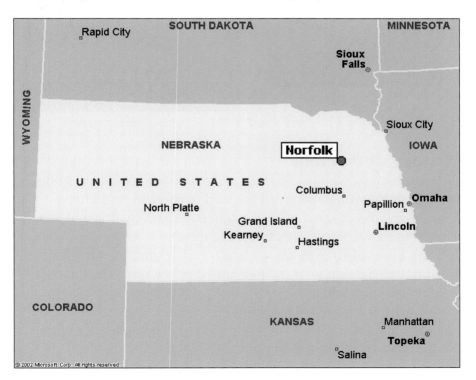

Norfolk City
Madison County
Nebraska State, U.S.A.

Administration: Mayor and eight Council Members.
Population: 24,000.
Norfolk has 18 Schools, 35 churches (and almost that number of denominations), 12 public parks, and some 70 organisations and seven radio stations.

One of the city parks

History of Norfolk

In 1866 some 44 German families and others from Wisconsin plus more from New England found the land to be good for farming
When one looks at some of the landing parts of New England it is not surprising that settlers were tempted to travel.
In 1881 a post office was named North Fork as part of that area. Norfork was thought to be simpler, and then the post office in their wisdom put the spelling right by calling it Norfolk – it seems that this story has been repeated elsewhere!
Highway and railway systems made Norfolk the largest city of the North Fork and Elkhorn valleys.

My visit in 1995

I very nearly never got to Norfolk NE as on the small plane the pilot turned to me and asked "Where are you going, buddy?" I replied "Norfolk." "Gee," he said, "we aren't going to any place called Norfolk." I showed him my itinerary and he said, "Sure, if you had told me NORFORK there would have been no problem. As it is I was about to turn round and take you back to where we started from!"

My visit of a mere one whole day and two half days was totally inclusive – from the meeting at the airport by City Administrator Michael Nolan and the subsequent full briefing – to the presentation of the "Golden Key of Norfolk NE" by Mayor Harley Rector. From the tours by Rick Benson (newspapers, radio, stores, vast beef slaughter organisation – some 2,000 head a day!), to talks to the Lions and a

Mayor Harley Rector presenting the City's "Golden Key"

7.30 a.m. church community "porridge" breakfast which was a great pleasure. My remark that "the porridge was very pleasant" caused great laughter – it was something called "grits" it seems....

I have many things noted with asterisks in my notebook, but one I'd like to mention is the cyclone shelter for an enormous grocery distribution centre – room for all and the "Ladies Rest Room" has an important place. We nearly had a cyclone alert while I was there!

Then of course the loss of my blazer in Winnipeg, left in the hired car in my early morning ice-laden rush. Delivered at Norfolk Airport later that afternoon....

Left: Rick Benson being "claimed" by the two Air Girls of Norfolk Airport after the collection of my recovered blazer!

Rick took me way out into the country and to the most exceptional site I had ever visited. It is the site where primeval animals have been discovered preserved in mountains of volcanic dust – it seems that this had been the result of a volcanic explosion way over in the west of the U.S.A. And to slake our thirst we visited a pioneering vineyard where no vineyard had ever been thought possible!

Norfolk Public Library. One of the most advanced of those I have visited, with fituristic facilities.

The commercial strength organisation as well as the citizen "togetherness"

Norfolk Police

My introduction to the Norfolk Police involved my being shown them introducing bicycle patrols with a demonstration of these being able to go up staircases!

Left: William L. Mizner. Appointed Chief of Police on August 24, 1987, becoming the 26th Chief of Police in the history of Norfolk Police.

Right: Norfolk NE Fire Chief (second from left) presenting his annual report which proved that his force had saved the city some $5 million by their services.

Norfolk, Nebraska's delegates to Norwich, Norfolk, England for the First International Family Gathering, standing outside the West Door of Norwich Cathedral.

And right, the Norfolk Nebraska State Flag being shown on Norfolk Island at our Second Gathering in 2000.

Quite reasonably, the question on that remote island was "Where is Norfolk Nebraska?" and while I explained with the aid of a map of U.S.A., I pointed out that the same question was on everyone's lips in that same Norfolk, Nebraska! "Where is Norfolk Island?"

Actually, Norfolk Island has connections with the U.S.A. as it is the only place outside the U.S.A. that celebrates Thanksgiving Day. This is due to the many American whaling ships that used to call in.

WORLD FAMILY

www.gurney.co.uk/norfolk

Norfolk   Norwich

New York State
U.S.A.

The New York State Flag

On a dark blue field is the State Coat of Arms. On the left, the goddess Liberty holds a pole with a Liberty cap on top. At her feet is a discarded crown, representing freedom from England at the end of the revolutionary war. On the right is the goddess, Justice. On the shield a sun rises over the Hudson highlands and ships sail the Hudson River. Above the shield is an eagle resting on a globe representing the Western Hemisphere.

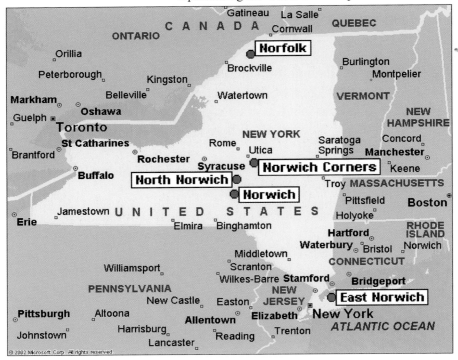

Norwich City and Norwich Town
Chenango County
New York State, U.S.A.

Administration: Council President, Mayor, and six Aldermen.
Population: 8,000.
Location: 42°31'52"N 75°31'26"W.

Background to Norwich City, NY

Excerpts from contribution of Kathryn L. Barton, historian

Norwich is located in central
New York State in the County
of Chenango and is the main
county city. The name Chenango
means land of the Bull Thistle
(the county flower).
Norwich is named after that U.S.
original Norwich, Connecticut,
an influence of so many of the

nation's other Norwiches. There is thence a direct connection with
Norwich England and "Nor'wich" is the usual pronunciation.

Norwich was settled in 1788 by one Avery Powers and finally became
a city in 1914 – since when there have been 18 Mayors, with the first
lady Mayor being Marjorie Chomyszak in her repeated two-year
terms of 1990 to 1994.

119

Extensive canals, main railway junctions and finally an airport have all emphasised the city's importance. Business has ranged from the basic necessities to large pharmaceutical connections. Nothing is permanent in these aspects and there have been catastrophic changes from time to time.

The schools, churches, libraries, museums and associations in Norwich are thriving as is the very energetic chamber of commerce.

Norwich's attractive tree-lined streets have many imposing houses of varying architecture.

There are many days in the year for citizens to celebrate particular aspects.

(Kathryn Barton's history of Norwich City, New York is available in Norwich UK USAAF Library)

The 1993 visit

My visit in 1993 was to a very warm welcome by Mayor Marge Chomyszak...

Left: Presenting the Norwich City UK Coat of Arms

My outstanding memory is of being instructed to stop at a village outside Norwich and to telephone the police station – where upon two vast police cars roared up, sandwiched my small dirty red car between them and made a much heralded light-flashing entrance into the city and to the Chomyszak house!

Above: The Court House with its notice of the first log cabin

Presentation to Marylou Stewart when she was Chairman of that most impressive Chamber of Commerce during my 1993 visit

Amongst some five opportunities to talk about my own Norwich with slides there was one class of children who had extra excitement in that my slide projector decided to create a fire! Later that day when given the opportunity to talk to the Rotary Club a sheaf of letters was delivered and these were from each one of that class

– some sympathising and hoping I would not get into trouble and one with lateral thinking saying that it was hard to imagine the English population of 52 million people on such a small island. "It appears that no one has room to lie down!"
When one realises the age of those children it is evident that Norwich NY has some very useful citizens in the making!

Norwich City, New York at the First Gathering
NORWICH CITY, UK 1996

Left: Norwich UK historian Center: Marge and Jerry Chomyszak – Right: Betty Distil (Betty had a Norwich pen friend from the Second World War until recently). Some 20 communities were represented (and then only some 30 had been found by that time!) and Marge played a full part!

Left: On board the Norwich Union coach in the Lord Mayor's procession

And right: Persuading the Bishop of Norwich to sign a memento world map – gently

North Norwich
Chenango County
New York State, U.S.A.

Administration: Supervisor and Town Board.
Population: 2,000.
Location: 42°37'1"N 75°31'38"W.

Right: Historian and co-author of that remarkable book "Next Stop Galena", Janet (Whaley) Decker and her team.

The following extract of the history of Norwich is taken from that book.

The story of North Norwich

North Norwich is located in Chenango County in central New York State. Our roots go back to 1792 when hardy pioneers braved the unbroken forest to seek homes in the "west". Many of our pioneer ancestors moved to North Norwich from Amenia, Dutchess County, New York. Their ancestors had arrived in America earlier, landing in Connecticut. Descendants of several of the original settlers are still living in the town.

North Norwich is a quaint, small village with several old houses in the town that date back to the early 1800s.

Right: William Hodges House

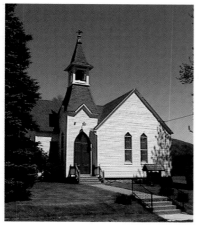

The town itself contains productive farms on scenic country roads, with some farms being kept in the same families for generations. Within the boundaries of the town of North Norwich are the hamlets of Plasterville, King's Settlement and Sherburne Four Corners.

Left: 150 year-old Methodist Church

Right: The Chenango Canal – one of the great communication ways

Amongst the many transportations along this canal was that of the 114th Regiment southwards to the Civil War, and at conclusion of that war they were brought home, those that survived. It was ironic that it was the Chenango Canal that brought the first railway engine to the valley and thus brought about its own demise.

From the first railway service via the Albany and Susquehanna company (1851) to the Conrail consolidation in 1970, the railway was the lifeline to the Chenango Valley. But the line was finally sold in 1982.

Advertising the town's 150th birthday celebration in 1999

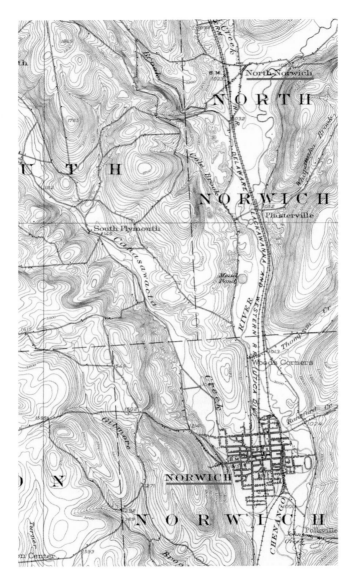

1910 map showing Norwich and North Norwich

East Norwich
Nassau County
New York State, U.S.A.

Population: 2,717.
Location: 40°50'48"N 73°32'8"W.

Our story of this research for all the communities in the world named either Norfolk or Norwich really begins here in East Norwich with Dorothy Horton McGee, her response to my first enquiries and her invitation to speak to my mission in 1993.

Dorothy took an immense risk in that we had never met before and I would like to think that it was justified – save for the fact of my deafness not allowing me to hear the British National Anthem so that Dorothy had it played again after warning me!

Supervisor and Mrs Lewis J. Yevoli, and on the right Dorothy Horton McGee at the presentation of my first ever Citation

About East Norwich

East Norwich is part of the Oyster Bay complex on the north shore of Long Island. It has a jealously guarded community spirit with its committees for beautification, its campaign for tidiness and its overall "village" atmosphere. A seat of history closely connected with the British in those early independence days....

Each year more than 200,000 Long Islanders and visitors from near and far participate in the region's largest street festival: a weekend of family fun, food and festivities hosted by the Oyster Bay Chamber of Commerce.

The history of East Norwich

Originally inhabited by the Matinecock Indians, Oyster Bay was settled and named (primarily due to its abundance of shellfish) by the Dutch in 1615.

Map of East Norwich in 1873

In the 1650s English settlers began arriving and starting communities a few miles inland. Amongst those who came to these shores were James and George Townsend from Norfolk UK (it is unknown if other Norfolk UK people came with them). Sometime towards the end of the seventeenth century, the name Norwich was chosen as the name of a settlement a few miles south of Oyster Bay. It wasn't until 1862 that the name was changed to East Norwich.

128

In Oyster Bay is the home of the Townsends, Raynham Hall (now a museum), which served as a British headquarters during the Revolutionary War, and can lay claim to a truly historic "first" – it is the home of America's first documented Valentine. On  February 14 over 200 years ago, Lt. Col. John Graves Simcoe of the Queens Rangers asked Sarah "Sally" Townsend to "choose me for your Valentine!"

Lisa Cuomo, the Education Coordinator at the museum has been very generous in giving the outlines of history and the remarkable Townsend family history concerning the East Norwich–British connections of the beginning of the United States of America and the pleasant concoction of the Great Chain story.

Of course no history of Oyster Bay would be complete without mentioning that most famous resident, and the only President from Long Island – Theodore Roosevelt, who built Sagamore Hill in Cove Neck in 1885.

Did you know Theodore Roosevelt is the only President of the U.S.A. to both win the Medal of Honor and be awarded a Nobel Prize?

During my visit, Paul Moreno gave great encouragement in promising to send the book on The History of East Norwich, and suggested to his School Principal that a student project on all these namesake communities could be of constructive interest.

East Norwich – 1910

East Norwich visits Norwich UK

Dorothy McGee came to Norwich England for the first ever gathering of the World Norfolk and Norwich Communities.

Huguette my wife and the East Norwich delegation at our 900 year old Cathedral.

Dorothy said that she had been surprised at the shortness of the flight from New York and then we discovered she had come by Concorde!
Such was the importance of this visit that the Norwich Town Crier took responsibility.

His Worship the Lord Mayor of Norwich UK accepted the Oyster Bay flag.

This was also on display at the Second World Gathering on Norfolk Island, South Pacific, 2000

Our second visit to East Norwich

In 1999 a delegation from Norwich UK visited East Norwich.
Dorothy McGee received the "Family Plaque" for the World Family
of Norfolk and Norwich on behalf of East Norwich.
Dorothy even had a "welcome cake"
for us!

And then Ken Rowe
presented the Delegation's
"streamer".

A sad note to end this chapter. Dorothy Horton McGee passed away
in 2003. She is buried with her parents in Arlington Cemetery.

Norwich Corners
Herkimer County
New York State, U.S.A.

Location: 43°0'52"N 75°12'45"W.

Yet another Norwich in New York State that is still shown on maps. Little is known as yet, but it was once a community. Now just a few houses from what we have found out so far. There once was a one-room school (shown right), that in 1945 had 27 pupils, with one teacher taking all six grades.

Another location that needs further exploration....

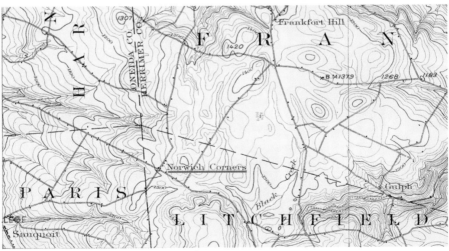

Norwich Corners on a 1910 map

Norfolk
St Lawrence County
New York State, U.S.A.

Administration: Supervisor and Council.
Population 4,700.

The Norfolk NY community was represented in Norwich, Norfolk, England at that first ever gathering in 1996 by a number of their residents led by the Hon. Patricia Fanning, assisted by Malcolm Starks, Library Chairman, Vicky Brothers, librarian and Leon Burnap, photographing historian. The delegation was attended by Carol Robinson, a Norwich City, UK cultural guide. They were taken to a memorial placed by Norwich citizens in memory of one of their own who as part of an aircraft crew based in Norfolk and a part of that large contingent of American airmen, had avoided crashing into a Norwich housing estate, but subsequently lost their lives in so doing.

Representatives of Norfolk NY at the first Family Gathering,
Norwich, Norfolk, England, 1996

Hon. Patricia Fanning giving a presentation at that first world gathering of the Norfolk and Norwich World Family, 1996 in Norfolk County Hall, England. (That figure bending over on the left is a delighted organiser looking at the clock and its dedication that had been presented to him – and which now is in the permanent organisational office, a reminder of Norfolk Community, New York State.)

My visit to Norfolk, NY

The overall contact arrived via Vicky Brothers and her management of Hepburn Library – in fact as the result of my self-invited visit. I was very impressed to see a map set up in the library with an arrow showing where the UK Norfolk and Norwich are, and there was Vicky showing some visiting children where this "foreigner" lived.

Above: Vicky Brothers and 'her' Library!

The Hepburn Library of Norfolk, New York, built in 1921 is one of seven Hepburn Libraries in Saint Lawrence County. The libraries were made possible by the generous donation of A. Barton Hepburn. Libraries were just one of many projects of this philanthropist. The towns of Colton, Edwards, Herman, Lisbon, Madrid, Norfolk and Waddington, New York are homes of the historic brick and stone libraries. The building still houses the original oak furniture.

I stayed with Vicky and her family whilst being given a tour of Norfolk – the mills, the museum, the administration, and some of those vast and impressive water control works on their international rivers. I met supervisors, church potentates, school teachers and politicians from amongst the community when entertained to a most enjoyable dinner. In some small recompense I was allowed to present a short talk on my own Norwich City and Norfolk County communities and received the inevitable question as to where in this world they might be.

There was an excellent contrast to this question when talking to the community of Norwich in the same state of New York. I mentioned Norfolk NY and there again the question was raised as to where it might be! A mere odd hundred mile away! This is yet another justification for my research and joining all our communities into this remarkable "World Family", the largest such family of namesakes internationally.

Probably the main celebration day is that of Labor Day when everyone gets into the act....

From left to right, church, museum, church, and Council

Charmers all and some sing!

There are 62 churches and one synagogue within 16 miles of Norwood. There are five churches located within Norwood and the First Presbyterian Church at Daily Ridge is just outside Norwood.

The singing clergyman and his
church, dedicated to St Andrew

History of Norfolk

Located along the Racquette River,
between Potsdam and Massena, the
town of Norfolk was established on
April 9, 1823, by dividing the Town
of Louisville in half. Norfolk became
a separate township of 35,500 acres
and 108 inhabitants. The boundaries
changed in 1834 when a section of
Stockholm was added, and again in
1844 when a portion was returned
to Louisville.The township saw quick growth and became a major
blue-collar community of saw mills, paper mills, grist mills and
woollen factories. Today, the town of Norfolk remains a paper mill
community with a population of 4,700 people, making Norfolk the
sixth largest population center in St Lawrence County.

There are four electric power dams on the Racquette River as the
river drops some 77 feet, and this is the basis for running the various
mills of Norwich.

There were originally four paper mills and there remains the one
– still using the same machinery. Many Hungarian families moved to

make up the mill work force and while their descendants still live in the town few still work there.

Today the main places of employment are the APC paper mill, the Highway Dept, the Barrett Stone quarry, the Museum and the Fire Department/Rescue Squad.

Between 1817 and 1867 the churches of Norfolk came into existence, firstly the First Congregational followed by the Grace Episcopalian Church, the Methodist Episcopalian Church, and finally the Roman Catholic Church. While the Wesleyan Church later took the building of the First Congregational Church, today there are also the Berean Baptist Church and the North Country Bible Church, which latter meet in the Heburn Library.

Norfolk, New York State is a really wholesome community!

One of my delights has been in receiving letters from some of the school students of Norfolk NY....

Hello England students. My name is James McGrath. My life in Norfolk is really fun. I have friends everywhere on my street.
A lot of the houses I think are very much alike. I love to go to the most funest library you can think of. The owner of it is Miss Vicky. She is really funny a lot. Every day is like an adventure to me. I live right down the road from a video store. I walk to the library everyday. Miss Vicky has published some of my books that I write. I write most about my friends.
Miss Vicky lets people read the books I write. Most of my friends say that it is a ghost town but I think that it is just great. What its more than great – it's fantastick. It must be great were you live too. My town has the most funest named streets you can even think of.
I love living in Norfolk, New York
Well that's all I know about. bye!
James McGrath, Age. 10, Norwood Norfolk School
Norfolk NY

About Norfolk

Do you have favorite things in your town? I do in my town. I live in
Norfolk, New York in the United States. I am 6 years old and my
name is Bekkah.
I like the Norfolk Fire Department, because I like the fire trucks.
We have three fire stations!
I like the softball field where my family plays ball during the
summer. I like watching them and I like playing on the Big green
bleachers.
Our playground has some horses that you ride and they rock. I like
those too. But my favorite part about Norfolk is that I live near four
of my friends and my Nana and Papa live next door!
Rebekkah C. Bond, age 6
Norwood-Norfolk Central School
Grade 1
Norfolk, NY

Norfolk is the 6th biggest town (population) in St. Lawrence County
in New York state.
We have 6 churches. 1 baptist church, 2 catholic churches, 2
united methodist churches, and one wesleyan church!!
The wesleyan church is right next to the library where there is
computers & reading material. There's an elementary school
where we learn how to read and to do mathematics, and
technology.
We also have a volunteer fire dept. and rescue squad. There are
32 towns in St. Lawrence county and Norfolk is the only town
that has a police dept.
There are few local stores in norfolk. Some of them are Al Smith's
superette, which has been owned by the same family for over 90
years. There is also Fefees market.
Norfolk has the only hungarian restaurant in the area, called

Sabads. There is also a mexican restaurant that is in a historic hotel. It is called the Hotel Grande.
There is a river that runs behind our house, it runs through the whole town. That is why there used to be 3 paper mills in our town. There is only one left. My grand father and great grandfather and most of my uncles worked in the papermills.
The most famous person to come from Norfolk was William P. Rogers. He was the secretary of state and secretary of the United States tresury for President Nixon. There is a street in our town named for his family called Rogers Drive. A lot of our streets are named for famous people, Wheeler Lane is named for a favorite town doctor, Hepburn Street is named for the man that gave money to build our library, Raymond Street and Atwater Street after one of the early settlers and Remington Ave. after the man who built the biggest paper mill.

Jarrett Bond, age 9.75
Norwood-Norfolk central school

Norfolk Fire Station, and the big brass sound from the firemen!

Ohio State
U.S.A.

The Ohio State Flag

The Ohio burgee, as the swallowtail design is properly called, was adopted in 1902. The large blue triangle represents Ohio's hills and valleys, and the stripes represent roads and waterways. The 17 stars symbolise that Ohio was the seventeenth state admitted to the Union. The white circle with its red center not only represents the "O" in Ohio, but also suggests Ohio's famous nickname, "the Buckeye State".

140

Norwich Township
Franklin County
Ohio State, U.S.A.

Administration: Board of Trustees.
Population: 4,000.
Area: 4 square miles.

Left to right: Trustees
Chuck Buck, Jim Rice,
Durland Workman and
Clerk Linda Gill

The Township originally was a part of
Franklin City but when Washington was
organised in 1809 it became a township in its
own right. And even more so in 1820. There
was no post office until 1852 and thus trade
and mail necessitated travelling great distances.

The first school was in 1814 and the first post office was in 1852
It appears that the name of Norwich came from Norwich Connecticut
and amongst many stories of danger was that of Peter Latimer,
born in Connecticut, who subsequently grew up and married in
Pennsylvania where he and his wife escaped marauding Indians by
lying between tree trunks and listening to the Indians looking for
them. In 1811 they emigrated to Norwich Ohio and he carried mail
from nearby Columbus to Zanesville (next to that Norwich Village).
He lived to the age of over 98 and his family of eight children all
lived locally.

Then another, Samuel Davis, was a spy against the Indians and
managed to escape when taken prisoner ... however his companion at
that time was eventually sold to the French after which he eventually
gained his freedom. They were tough times!

141

The township has its own fire service which is, to say the least, comprehensive as it deals not only with fires but also all the possible consequences from first aid to hospitalisation.

Churches were firstly Wesley Methodist and others include the Methodist Episcopal Church whilst there were the societies of Odd Fellows from 1867 and a Masonic Lodge from 1873.

The story of a past resident
(from an old print)

The subject of this sketch, Mrs Emula Rogers, was born in Connecticut, November 22, 1799. Her father and mother were Abner and Mercy Gillett Clapp. When about 6 years of age, her parents removed to Martinsburg, Lewis County, New York, where she passed her early life, and where she obtained a good education for that early day. She was married October 12, 1823, to Asa Moore Rogers, by whom she raised three children – Mary, Lester Asa, and Julia E. Her husband died January 2, 1831, and

on September 16, 1835, she was again married. Her choice fell on Apollos Rogers, a brother of her former husband. By him she had two children – twins – to whom they gave the names of Eli and Ela. Mr Rogers, her husband, had been married previously, and had several children by his first wife.

In 1836, with their family, they emigrated to Ohio, arriving in Norwich Township, September 29th of that year. Mr. Rogers bought a farm near the Scioto River and well toward the southern line of the township, where two of his sons – Marcellus and Milton Rogers – lived after him. Here he died, September 17, 1840. Mrs Emula Rogers, his wife, survived him, and died February 9, 1871, aged 71 years.

Of her children, Lester A. moved to Grand Rapids, Michigan, where he continued to live. Julia E. lived singly in California. Mary married John Howard, July 4, 1850, and lived in Norwich Township. Their home was about eight miles from Columbus, on the River Road.

Tales of Times Past

Justice as it was...

The Justice of the Peace was called upon to settle a dispute concerning a cross dog which was owned by an important farmer.

He accused another of shooting his dog and witnesses testified that they had seen this farmer with a gun. The Justice considered so long that the dog owner became impatient. Finally the Justice said "I do fine the plaintiff. I shot the dog myself. It needed doing!"

Norwich Township
Huron County
Ohio State, U.S.A.

Administration: Three trustees and a clerk.
Population: 1,200.
Area: 26 square miles.

The history of Norwich Township

The township was named after its Connecticut namesake and at the original survey it contained 16,529 acres and the land was valued to the original grantees at $1.50 per acre.

From 1808 to the end of the 1812 war many of the grantees had sold or left their land to heirs.

The first road was made by the men of General Beall's army in 1812. A survey of that trail shows where it crossed the later B & O railway.

Sections were surveyed into 100 acre lots and a village was laid out... the latter was never occupied save for the skeleton of the village house. This was named Barbados and now there is a village named Havana ... one wonders at the possible connections.

The first surviving birth was in 1817 and the first marriage was in 1819. The first frame building was a barn in 1832 and then the first house in that style was built in 1835 but unfortunately it soon burned down, to be followed by a brick-built home.

The post office was named North Norwich so as not to be confused with that of Norwich, Muskingum County and the first postmaster was there for some 20 years.

The first corn (maize) and wheat were grown in 1817.

The first school house was built in 1819 and consisted of a bare oak log cabin covered in elm bark – only split oak benches and the windows were cracks between the log walls.

In 1827 the first elections were at great risk because on the return journey from Norwalk the two yoke ox wagon overturned in the river and the ballot box had to be rescued by diving in and collecting it before it was washed away.

Deer, coon skins and beeswax were the main money spinners but at one time there were some five stores in the neighbouring areas and gradually the winding tracks could be called roads where teamsters drove their six horse teams with immense wagons called "land schooners".

The soil is loam and the subsoil brick clay – all well adaptable to

agriculture whilst the township was heavily wooded at the outset. Today the land is well fenced and farmed and 90 per cent own their own homes, stock yards and grain barns.

Left: Huron County Fair – a familiar picture in all county fairs worldwide!

Willard is the largest community in the township, and it is from the generosity of their librarian Beverly R. Brandt that much of this information has been gathered.

Norfolk   Norwich

Norwich Village
Muskingum County
Ohio State, U.S.A.

Administration: Mayor (part time).
Population: 500.

The village has a post office, two
churches, Presbyterian and United
Methodist, sharing a preacher with
other communities, and four stores.

History of Norwich
by kind donation of John and Doris Allen

Prior to the opening of the "Zane Trace" the area was one of Indian
settlements and the names of the first pioneers will ever remain
unknown as they pushed still further into the wilds of the Great West.
There were many families that sought to try their fortunes further
West and contingents came from Philadelphia as well as other Eastern
areas.
The early prosperity of Norwich was due to the National Road that
was ordained by George Washington and Thomas Jefferson. This was
the first federally supported road in U.S. history.

In 1827 William Harper of Norwich, England bought land from John
Crawford along the proposed new highway and laid out a town and
called it Norwich. Harper, a bachelor, did not remain long as he had
problems with some of the inhabitants and left for England.
Today the National Road is a quieter alternative to the roaring

interstate nearby. Although some sections have been abandoned most of it remains intact and links the small towns that prospered along its historic way.

There is however a further international fame in Norwich's housing the Zane Grey Museum.
All those who have been immersed in the stories of the Wild West cowboy days

would do well to make this a site for pilgrimage!
Zane Grey was probably the most famous of those authors.
Zane Grey's ancestor, Colonel Ebenezer Zane, was commissioned by the Continental Congress to develop a road through the Western Wilderness (Pennsylvania and Ohio at the time).

This museum has three main sections: the National Road, Zane Grey, and Ohio pottery (the area is well known for the quality of pottery made locally).
The Zane Grey section has numerous items of interest including books, movie posters, fishing items, and several recreations of Zane Grey settings.

We are indebted to Mr Alan Clark, the Museum Director for contacts in the village of Norwich.

Pennsylvania State U.S.A.

The Pennsylvania State Flag

Pennsylvania's State Flag is composed of a blue field on which the State Coat of Arms is embroidered. Draft horses are on either side of the Coat of Arms and the American eagle rests on the top. The scroll at the bottom reads "Virtue, Liberty and Independence".
The first State Flag bearing the State Coat of Arms was authorized by the General Assembly in 1799.

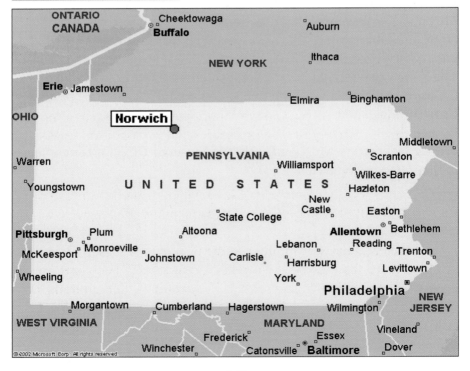

148

Norwich Township
McKean County
Pennsylvania State, U.S.A.

Administration: Supervisor and Secretary/Treasurer
(Patricia C. Fay – who has kindly provided information).
Population: 633.
Area: 96 square miles.

Norwich Township is in a remote area of
the state and mainly forested mountains up
to 2,200 feet above sea level. The whole
of McKean County is now part of the
Allegheny National Forest Region.
There are no major towns in the township.
There are two churches in the villages

of Volegroive and Crosby, and the school pupils are bussed to the
nearest town – Smethport – some 7 miles away in Keating Township.

Early history
In the early 1800s, word spread of land being available in the thick
timberlands full of wild game in McKean County, Pennsylvania.

One of the chief early migrations to the new county was in October of
1815 when 15 families from Norwich, Connecticut, came to the area
by way of Norwich, NY and settled. They followed Indian trails, and
had to cut their way through the forests to make a path for the wagons
and carts.

The heads of families that led this migration were: Abbey, Brewer, Burdick, Burlingame, Colegrove, Comes, Gallup, Irons, Smith and Wolcott.

We are indebted to Carlyn Gallup Seighman, author of the book "Rememberance" which is an amazing history of the Gallup family, for her stoies and photographs; and to Ross Porter who is the scholastic authority on the area and has also provided information.

Those early pioneers had to provide for themselves, clearing the land, building their own houses, and turning their hand to any job that needed doing. Before the roads were built. the best way to travel was by the many creeks through the area. In fact for a short time the creeks were designated as public highways!
Carlyn Seighman recalls a charming tale about her grandfather, a schoolteacher, who in the winter would put his skates on and skate down Potato Creek to the school!

An old photograph of Betula, Norfolk Township
nicely illustrating how the American term "sidewalk" came about

Norwich
Mckean County
Pennsylvania State, U.S.A.

Population: ?
Location: 41°39'34"N 78°22'25"W.

When the first Norwich settlers arrived in the county in 1815 there were few established settlements. Smethport, today the largest town in the area, had just two families living there. The Norwich group moved south a few miles, bought land alongside Potato Creek, felled the trees, built cabins and cleared the land, and the villages of Norwich and Betula were born.

One can only marvel at the courage and versatility of these early pioneers. Carlyn Seighman, in her book "Remembrance", tells the story of this fine house (right) built by the Kimble family. Later the house was jacked up and a basement put underneath. And even then it wasn't finished! Much late still, they cut the roof off, jacked it up under stilts, and built a second story.

By 1890 there was a road system, and the villages were getting nicely established. For the next 20 years the communities slowly developed, unaware of the drastic changes that were about to happen....

In 1909, the railway line was extended to Norwich, and the next year the Goodyear Lumber Co. moved in with a huge sawmill, and Norwich quickly grew into a town of 5,000 as the lumber company stripped the area of its native hemlock and hardwoods.

Left: Part of Norwich during the boom years
Below: Norwich School

Even though this was planned as being only a 10-year operation, nothing was spared in building the community. Churches and schools were built, and an array of shops and businesses flourished for a while – until Charles Hull built the Norwich Department Store – the largest store in northwestern Pennsylvania.

A massive building which sold anything and everything, employed two tailors, and even had overhead electric cash carriers that took your money up to the office and returned with your change. Before long, several of the smaller businesses in the area were going bankrupt.

A while later, the Department Store burnt down in suspicious circumstances....

Two views of Norwich Department Store

152

10 years later, 26,000 acres had been cleared of timber and the company moved its mills, employees and their houses to another area. The railway line was removed, and Norwich became a ghost town.

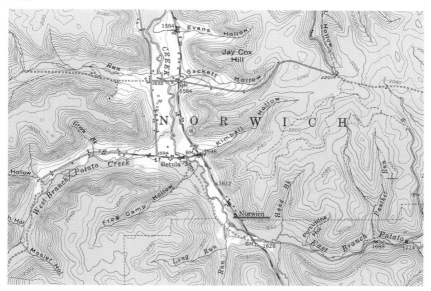

This 1948 map shows what little was left of Norwich and Betula after the timber company moved out. The junction above Betula was known as Norwich Corners.

Below: The same house in the 1800s and in 2003!
Our thanks to Carlyn Gallup Seighman for the photographs.

Vermont State
U.S.A.

The Vermont State Flag

A deep blue field contains a shield. The picture on the shield is a scene painting. You see a tall pine tree, a cow and sheaves of wheat. The Green Mountains are in the distance. Pine boughs extend around a shield. The name "Vermont" and the state motto "Freedom and Unity" are displayed on a crimson banner. At the top of the shield is a stag's head.

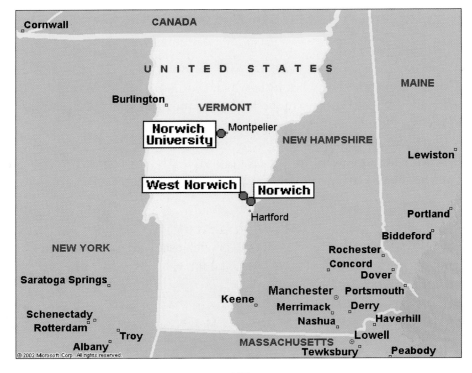

154

Norwich and West Norwich
Windsor County
Vermont State, U.S.A.

Administration: Board of Selectmen.
Population: 3,500.
Location: 43°42'55"N 72°18'30"W.

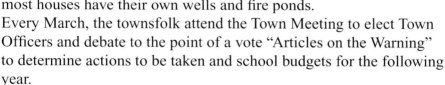

Town of Norwich, Vermont

CHARTERED 1761

Norwich is a town of volunteers. The Town Committees, the Fire Department are all volunteers. There is no mains water system but most houses have their own wells and fire ponds.

Every March, the townsfolk attend the Town Meeting to elect Town Officers and debate to the point of a vote "Articles on the Warning" to determine actions to be taken and school budgets for the following year.

The Town Library has recently been enlarged. It is computer compliant for both staff and customers.

Then there are those very active service organisations, the Lions, the Norwich Women's Club, the Grange and the American Legion.

Norwich history

On July 4 1761, the proprietors of Norwich received a charter and came up from Mansfield, Connecticut each spring to clear selected lots of land.

In 1765 a committee of five laid out the road system and that year the first two non-native families came up the Connecticut River by canoe, built log cabins and survived their first rugged winter.

Today Norwich is a delightful village with beautiful wooded hills, far views and pasture land. The Green Mountains, Vermont State's "backbone" are within easy reach, with their ski areas, lakes and wilderness scenery. This is a winter and summer recreation area with the benefit of nearby Dartmouth College.

There is a population of some 3,500 with many working in Hanover, a mile away, at the college or medical school. But there is a growing emphasis on computer software development and working from home is becoming popular.
There is also the tendency for large attractive retirement houses being built, whilst the high standard of education is another attraction.

Norwich, Vermont delegation at the First Family Gathering, Norwich, Norfolk, UK, 1996

My visit in 1993

My world exploratory cycle included Norwich Vermont in 1993, and as I had time I drove through and over the hills. I stopped at a farm with calves being reared in their own little insulated huts under the most modern methods and congratulated the farmer – who seemed surprised.

Then back to Norwich (or was it West Norwich?), and on the hill overlooking the town was a timber bungalow with two "old" lads sitting in the garden sunning themselves....
I stopped and passed the time of day. One called Bill and the other John said that theirs was the original site of Norwich before the railway came, and proved it by a map. Then I was taken to the back of the bungalow and over the hill to a graveyard. There were graves of those who had downed tools to fight the British in 1776 – that year was so marked on the slate headstones. This was the most poignant memory I had in all my journeys – those lads had gone off – been killed and their relatives had brought them all the way back home. The mind goes blank at the thought of that journey – no roads and a slow grieving cart....

Arriving at the centre of "modern" Norwich I was met by John Lawe and I remarked upon his excellent English accent. "I am English", he said!
I explained that I still hadn't found the handbrake to my hired car – after some five days of driving! He solved this with one press of his foot on a lever!!!

My reception was one of great generosity. From the introduction to the Selectmen government, to a tour of the College Campus and system explanation, to the meeting of some delightful personalities to a great "bring a dish" supper.

My day and a half was most rudely ended by my sneaking off at an early hour next morning from John and Jean Lawe's house for the journey to Norwich, New York State.

I left a piece of me in Norwich Vermont! That piece is with Jean and John whose help with "Our Family" has been enormously appreciated! My visit in 1993 was the beginning!

Right: Jean and John Lawe whose support has been the foundation, and are

my main and extremely helpful contacts. (Also appreciated is the fact that John showed me where the car brake was!)

John (right) all the way from Norwich VT to Norfolk Island, South Pacific for the Second World Gathering in 2000!
(in the center – he's not angry! only lost his notes!!!)

WEST NORWICH
Location: 43°45'48"N 72°22'24"W.

The Beaver Meadow Union Chapel stands in picturesque isolation in
the rural hamlet of Beaver Meadow (West Norwich), approximately
5.4 miles north-west of Norwich, VT. Constructed in 1915.
As has been the tradition with most New England religious structures
since the late nineteenth century, the Beaver Meadow Union Chapel
is painted white. (Butler, "Another City upon a Hill" : 31)

(from an 1895 Atlas)

Norwich University
Washington County
Vermont State, U.S.A.

In 1819, Captain Aldridge Partridge founded the American Literary, Scientific, and Military Academy in Norwich, Vermont. Captain Partridge had designed a novel system of education which combined civilian and military studies in order to produce enlightened and useful civilian soldiers.

The fundamental promise was that eduction must prepare youth for the responsibilities of peace and war.

Aldridge Partridge
(1785–1854)

The Academy was unique in its concept and development. It included modern languages, history, political economy, engineering,

civil engineering and agriculture in its curriculum. In 1825, the Academy moved to Middletown, Connecticut, but when it failed to get a charter it moved back to Norwich. In 1834 the Academy received a charter from the State of Vermont recognizing the institution as Norwich University. By this time many other private institutions had been established across the U.S.A. following Partridge's principles.

In 1866, the South Barracks at Norwich burned down, and Norwich University moved to its current location in Northfield, just south of the State Capital at Montpelier.

Virginia State U.S.A.

The Virginia State Flag

A deep blue field contains the Seal of Virginia with the Latin motto "Sic Semper Tyrannis" – "Thus Always to Tyrants". Adopted in 1776. The two figures are acting out the meaning of the motto. Both are dressed as warriors. The woman, Virtue, represents Virginia. The man is holding a scourge and chain which shows that he is a tyrant. His fallen crown is nearby.

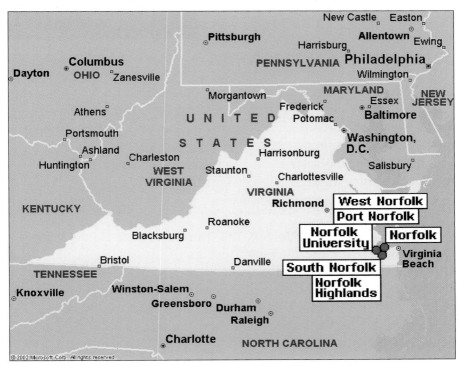

Norfolk City
Virginia State, U.S.A.

Population: 261,229.
Administration: Council of seven non-partisan Councillors headed by a Mayor.
Location: 36°50'48"N 76°17'8"W.

Norfolk City, Virginia, could well be the best-known Norfolk in the world. It is certainly the largest of the world Norfolk cities.

There is a well established relationship with Norfolk County UK – if sometimes desultory – but there is a continuing exchange of choral and individual contacts, wherein our own World Norfolk and Norwich Family plays its part. The intention is to broaden these contacts between organisations and most especially between school pupils within this unique facility for the discovery of community backgrounds School contacts are being canvassed and UK communication exchange offered. We offer further contacts via our web site at www.gurney.co.uk/norfolk/

Located near downtown Norfolk and overlooking the Hague Inlet of the Elizabeth River, the Chrysler Museum of Art has been called "one of the pleasantest places in the United States to while the day away". The National Maritime Center is located on the downtown waterfront in Norfolk, Virginia. Home to the Battleship Wisconsin, Nauticus is an exciting 120,000 square-foot science and technology center exploring the power of the sea.

Norfolk, VA – Norfolk, UK connections

There are so many stories of connections with Norfolk, England, and just one is the tale of young Henry Spelman – son of the High Sheriff of Norfolk, England.

In 1608 when still a boy he was captured by Native Americans. His life was spared due to Princess Pocahontas (later Mrs Rolfe, who died in Norfolk England – yet another tale!).

Henry learned the natives' language and when freed became an interpreter to the governor. But then he was killed in a raid by the very people he had championed. There are church memorials in Narborough, Norfolk, England; but now no more Spelman family.

My visit in 1994

There are many reports of the generous welcome given to visitors and my own introductory visit was an outstanding case in point. Choirs are particularly prominent in exchanges largely due to an excellent relationship built up over the years.

Left: The 1996 gathering – the first World Gathering of world Norfolk and Norwich communities. Breck Daughtrey receiving a Norfolk County medal from the County Chairman of Norfolk County UK.

My experience was largely concerned with the Sister City Society and with typical generosity I was whisked from political meeting to real estate to luncheon with their President to City Hall, given the opportunity to give two talks, an impressive conducted city tour – all in a day and a half before catching my plane to another Norfolk and Norwich Family community.

Endearing memories always remain of a fabulous city that rose from the ashes of military destruction, yet today has the warmest of friendship and so many mutual interests with her English counterpart.

Right: Pin presentation of my home city to the Sister City stalwarts – all looking politely impressed with my minuscule gift!
What nice people they are!

Left: At one of the receptions. Lane Dare showing how the Greeks do it!

More about Norfolk

Norfolk City, amongst all its celebrations has that magnificent spring Azalea Festival – marked by their glorious Azalea Gardens and inaugurated to mark Norfolk U.S.A. as the Headquarters of NATO (the North Atlantic Treaty Organisation). Here in that vast naval base is that other Norfolk community – namely that of the USS Norfolk, whose response to an invitation to be with us in 1996 at that first of the newly discovered Family Gatherings in Norwich, Norfolk UK was "Regrets, but we shall be under the Antarctic ice at the time."

History of Norfolk
An introduction by Peggy Hale McPhillips

The English arrived in 1624 with land granted by King James I and then by King Charles I to Thomas Willoughby – some 700 acres in all. Another early settler, Adam Thoroughgood, christened the area "New Norfolk" after his home county.

The significance of Norfolk as a major port was when the Crown ordered storehouses to receive imported goods and tobacco for export. Norfolk was incorporated as a city in 1845.

In 1776 on New Year's Day, the Royal Governor, Lord Dunmore, ordered an attack on the then Borough of Norfolk and destroyed most of the early buildings – this was the only American town completely destroyed and then rebuilt by the end of the century. (A cannon ball in the wall of St Paul's Church is a historical reminder.)

Virginia surrendered to Federal troops and after the Civil War Norfolk became the greatest port in the world.
Norfolk City grew to its present size from the reorganisations between 1887 and 1959, and two world wars brought the population to its present, ever-growing size.

From 50 acres of land and a population of one, Norfolk has grown to 66 square miles and a population of more than 200,000.

(Full edition lodged in the Norwich USAAF library UK)

By the 1890s Norfolk was a thriving city and port, and just across the
Elizabeth River, two new Norfolks were being planned –
Port Norfolk and West Norfolk.

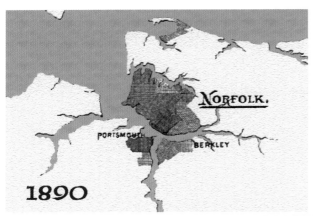

It's hard to believe
that these two sketch
maps (showing the
populated areas) are
only 110 years apart.

But, it does give us
three more Norfolk
communities to
check out....

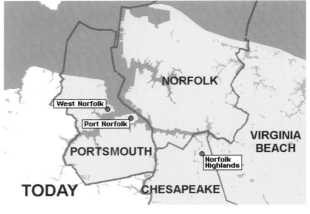

Norfolk State University
Norfolk
Virginia State, U.S.A.

Norfolk State College was founded in 1935. The college, brought to life in the midst of the Great Depression, provided a setting in which the youth of the region could give expressions to their hopes and aspirations.

Today, the university is proud to be one of the largest predominantly black institutions in the nation. Furthermore, it is committed to pursuing its vital role of serving the people of the Hampton Roads area.

Norfolk State University offers a remarkable balance between quality and cost. Students are able to receive the utmost in academic excellence without the worry of tuition being overpriced. Students find that NSU is worth the time, money, and effort. After all, college education is a big investment and NSU is definitely a great buy!

The university houses a fabulous and unique facility – the Lois E. Woods Museum – the gallery of which houses an extensive African art collection within its 10,000 square foot exhibit space, which represents 46 tribes within 14 African countries.

South Norfolk
Chesapeake
Virginia State, U.S.A.

South Norfolk was incorporated as a town in 1919. The City of Chesapeake was created with the merger of Norfolk County and the City of South Norfolk in 1963. The city's history dates back much further. Chesapeake is the site of the battle of Great Bridge which took place on December 9, 1775, just a few hundred yards from where City Hall stands today.

Chesapeake is also the site of the Great Dismal Swamp and the South Norfolk Historic District.

Chesapeake is in fact a community of communities, each with its own distinctive history, and South Norwich is a district that is struggling to keep its community identity alive.

Still very active is the South Norfolk Library.

The first South Norfolk Library was sponsored by the Women's Club of South Norfolk and opened its doors with a donated collection in Lakeside Park in 1953. In May 1956, the library moved to a rented

building at 1015 Chesapeake Avenue where it remained until 1958 when the building at the corner of Poindexter and Decatur Streets was constructed.

Linwood L. Briggs, Jr., as Mayor

of South Norfolk, was instrumental in proposing construction of the South Norfolk Library as a memorial to those who lost their lives in the Second World War. During his years of dedicated service, Mr Briggs collected historic photographs of South Norfolk.

On September 26, 1997, the literacy room was dedicated to Mr Linwood L. Briggs. Many of his collected historic photographs of South Norfolk are displayed in the History and Literacy Room.

Raymond L. Harper is the current historian whose researches have made a firm base for the memory and continued being of South Norfolk within the Chesapeake complex.

Norfolk Highlands
Chesapeake
Virginia State, U.S.A.

Population: ?
Administration: ?
Location: 36°48'56"N 76°13'56"W.

Another new discovery of which we know little. Internet searches have revealed it has a primary school, and we are hoping to make contact soon....

Norfolk Highlands gets its name from being the highest point of land in the area. Lying between the Indian River and the Virginia Beach city boundary, it still has the feel of the countryside about it. Houses started to appear in the 1950s when this was still farmland.

Port Norfolk
Portsmouth
Virginia State, U.S.A.

Population: ?
Administration: ?
Location: 36°50'54"N 76°20'8"W.

Port Norfolk is a turn of the century neighborhood in Portsmouth, Virginia, located on the southern shore of the Elizabeth River between Hull Creek and Pinners Point.
In 1890 a real estate syndicate developed Port Norfolk. To promote the new community a contest to name it was held and 12 lots were given away. Houses went up rapidly and with the streetcar connection from Portsmouth in 1893 the area became a popular resort location.

The area was advertised as a boating, fishing and swimming destination. A hotel, two piers, a bathhouse, gas lamps, and wooden sidewalks enticed visitors to the resort area.

Chesapeake Hotel, Port Norfolk – 1892

Left: Port Norfolk Fire Station c.1940

Our thanks to Richard Ivy for providing the photographs on these pages.

It is estimated that 80 percent of the homes were built between 1895 and 1920. The prevailing building style was vernacular Victorian with modified versions of Queen Anne, American Four Square, Colonial Revival, and Arts and Crafts. The Queen Anne with expansive wraparound porches, irregular roof lines, bays and turrets; the Four Square with cubic shaped hipped roof, dormers, broad front porch, little use of ornament, built in wood and brick; and the Arts and Crafts recognized by a low roof with wide eaves. Porches or verandas are often decorated as carefully as indoor rooms and enjoyed as outdoor sitting areas.

The neighborhood has re-tained much of its original charm and character, with shady tree-lined streets, a lovely waterfront, and a quaint business district. Port Norfolk takes on the charac-ter of a small town, all within the midst of the big city.

From the photographs we have seen, the Port Norfolk residents take a great pride in their community.

172

And there is a great community spirit as well. The following photographs show a project in December 2003 – a playground the neighborhood built with the help of a national material supply company. The neighborhood put in $20,000 (materials and insurance) and Home Depot put in $10,000 and supplied some heavy equipment and labor. The workers were half Port Norfolk residence and friends. The rest were from Home Depot.

Debbie Foytik (left with the sledge hammer) was the driving force and she had been raising money for 2½ years.

Right: Retiring President Richard Ivy and wife taking a break.

And finally, the Port Norfolk Gang! Congratulations to everyone involved.

West Norfolk
Portsmouth
Virginia State, U.S.A.

Population: ?
Administration: ?
Location: 36°51'50"N 76°20'59"W.

West Norfolk lies across the river from the city of Norfolk VA.
By the 1890s, West Norfolk was a developing community. It has been described as the place where sail met rail. Once a thriving community

with hotels, restaurants and train stations, it has declined over the years, and in 1895 was incorporated into the town of Portsmouth.

Today, it is a small community of about 200 homes, an industrial plant and two churches.

The West Norfolk Baptist Church can trace its beginnings back to 1891, when the Reverend A. B. Dunaway, pastor of Churchland Baptist, held services for the community of West Norfolk in a building on the waterfront. The church still in use today was built in 1900.

USS Norfolk
United States of America

The current USS Norfolk is a nuclear powered submarine with a complement of 12 officers and 98 enlisted men.

We invited the USS Norfolk to the first gathering of the Norfolk and Norwich World Family in 1996, and received a most polite reply: "Regretting our inability to be present as we should be under the Antarctic ice at the time!"

Before this submarine there was the destroyer Norfolk for which there is a very strong "old boys" organisation.

Western Australia State
Australia

The Western Australia State Flag

The flag of Western Australia is a British Blue Ensign defaced with the State Badge depicting the native black swan on a yellow disc, with the swan swimming towards the hoist.

The black swan has long been a symbol of Western Australia. The original colony was in fact called the Swan River Settlement. The flag was adopted in 1953.

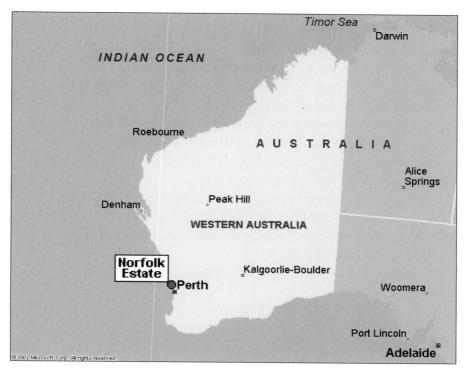

Norfolk Estate, Quinns Rocks
Western Australia
Australia

Population: ?
Administration: ?
Location: 31°45'S 115°43'E.

Quinns Rocks began as a coastal village approximately 35 km north of Perth, populated by retirees, holidaymakers and fishermen.

It takes its name from the offshore reef first noted during a coastline survey by Surveyor James Cowle in 1867. Although spelled with a double "n", the rocks are thought to have been named after Robert Quin who emigrated to Western Australia in 1863 and was appointed as an Assistant Surveyor on his arrival. Quin died in July 1886. The general area on the coast opposite the rocks was referred to as Quinns Rocks by the Wanneroo Road Board when they requested the survey of a road to that place in November 1925. Later the place also came to be called "Wanneroo Beach".

There was some pastoral activity in the general area sometime after 1860, with first official pastoral grants being issued in 1888. The first actual land title in the area was not given until 1940. Quinns Rocks was declared a townsite in 1962.

Norfolk Estate is a Landstart development project at Quinns Rocks.

(Our thanks to Alastair Honeybun, Administrator for most of this information)

About Norfolk Estate
by Hazel Cook

We are an estate in Quinns Rocks and I guess we came by the name through the developers of the estate. The estate is about 10 years old now. There are streets named after Norfolk Island and the "Mutiny on the Bounty", e.g. Christian Circle, Mutiny Terrace, and Pitcairn Entrance, to name a few.

This estate is part state housing, with a 1:12 ratio of "Homeswest" to private dwellings. We have many nationalities here. In our street we have Australian, Aboriginal, English, French, Maltese, Japanese, Afghan and Spanish. (Our Canadian neighbours moved last year!) It is a very interesting mix...

Left: Norfolk House. The house has been made available for community use and currently has craft groups, playgroups, various courses, and resident association meetings etc. being held there.

Right: Photo of a fun day which was held here. This man came with all kinds of kites and talked to the children about them and then they made some and flew them on Foundation Park, which is what you see pictured. It was actually so windy that he couldn't fly his big kites. And is that a Norfolk pine?

As you look at the photograph, imagine a 15-minute walk across the park and up the opposite street and you will come to the Indian Ocean, absolutely gorgeous.
What a privilege to live here!

Left: Quinns Beach Primary School.
The school has only been going for a couple of years.

As we go to print, we have heard of two estates near Brisbane called Norfolk and Norfolk Downs. Also of a parish of Norfolk and a parish of Norwich both in Queensland.
Norfolk parish comes under the City of Mt Isa
Norwich is listed as a parish in the Shire of Paroo.

If anyone 'down under' can help with providing more information on any of these communities we would be very grateful.

Tasmania
Australia

The Tasmanian Flag

The Fag of Tasmania is a British Blue Ensign
defaced with the State Badge. The badge depicts
a red lion passant on a white disc. The badge was
approved by the British Colonial Office in 1875
and the design of the Tasmanian Flag has remained
unchanged since then, save for a slight alteration
in the rendition of the lion in 1975 when the flag
was officially proclaimed as the "Tasmanian Flag".

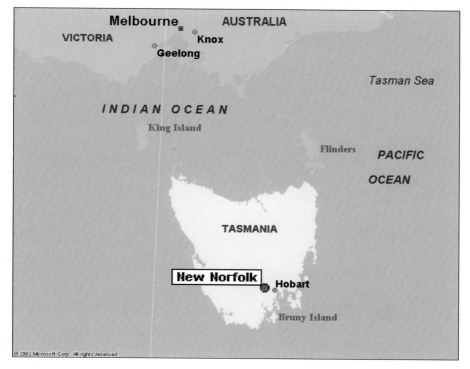

New Norfolk
Tasmania, Australia
Text and photographs by Damian Bester

Population: 5,300.
Administration: ?

Few places in Australia have a history to match the old town of New Norfolk. The first settlers in the district arrived soon after Europeans colonised Tasmania in 1803, but the town itself was not established until the first evacuees arrived from the abandoned Norfolk Island. But even when the Norfolk Islanders stepped off the Lady Nelson in November 1807, there was no Melbourne (settled 1835), Adelaide (1836), Brisbane (1825) or Perth (1829).

In its picturesque valley setting, the town of New Norfolk is famous as one of Australia's most scenic towns – as well as one of its oldest and most historic

The district was originally referred to as the Hills, but the settlers from Norfolk Island quickly adopted the name "New" Norfolk, and resisted later efforts by Governor Lachlan Macquarie to impose the name Elizabeth Town in honour of his wife.

Settlers lived on government rations until 1812 and the town's early growth was far from rapid. Visitors often remarked that the town had only a hotel and a church, both of which now rank among New Norfolk's list of Australia's "first" or "oldest" things. One of the Norfolk Island evacuees was Betty King, and her headstone in a local churchyard records that she was the first white woman to set foot in Australia.

The convict Denis McCarty became the district's first police constable in 1808, and in 1818 he was contracted to build the first arterial road in the colony, between Hobart and New Norfolk.

Under the Patronage of their Excellencies the Governors of Tasmania and adjacent Colonies.

⚜BUSH ● HOTEL,⚜
NEW NORFOLK.

The above Hotel (established over 70 years) is without exception one of the Best in the Island for Sanitary arrangements, and beautifully situated on the banks of the River Derwent, commanding some of the Grandest Scenery in the Australian Colonies.

All the Appointments of a First-class Hotel; also, Large Garden of choice Fruit and Flowers.

Boat, Bait, Fishing Tackle, &c., and civil Attendant to take charge of Fishing or Shooting Parties.

Visitors are respectfully requested to communicate direct with the Proprietor, as some self-interested people are in the habit of saying the house is full when such is often not the case.

Telegrams and Letters Promptly Attended to. Telephonic Communication with Hobart.

Carriages wait the arrival of Steamers to convey Visitors to and from Hotel, Free of Charge.

TERMS:—10s. per Day; or, £3 3s. per Week. Private Sitting Room Extra.

O. BLOCKEY,
Proprietor,

Despite rival claimants to the title, the Bush Inn Hotel (1825) is acknowledged as the oldest continually licensed hotel in Australia. Reverend Bobby Knopwood stood down from the Hobart chaplaincy in 1823 and retired to New Norfolk, where an Anglican church was being built. St Matthew's Church, while significantly altered over the years, remains as Tasmania's oldest church. Nearby, St Paul's Uniting Church (1835) is the oldest former Methodist church still in use in Australia.

The town had its own Government House and there were attempts to make New Norfolk the colonial capital until the idea was finally vetoed in 1826.

The New Norfolk Municipal Chambers is the seat of local government for the Derwent Valley Municipality, which includes a number of smaller towns and villages in addition to the main civic centre.

A convict hospital was established in 1827 and the barrack square now known as "Willow Court" was completed in 1831.

It became part of the Royal Derwent Hospital which, at the time of its closure in 2001, was Australia's oldest mental hospital still on its original site.

Governor Sir John Franklin laid a foundation stone at New Norfolk in 1840 on the intended site of Tasmania's first university. The stone did not last a day, as it was quickly dug up and hauled into the river by those who disagreed with the plan.

Hops were established at New Norfolk in 1846 and grew to become one of the Derwent Valley's most important industries. Smallholdings throughout the district have since given way to a centralised industry at Bushy Park which continues to supply the majority of hops needed to flavour and preserve the nation's beer supply.

The New Norfolk district is dotted with a number of timber oast houses, or hop-drying kilns, such as this one

The district became a rural municipality in 1863 and a year later Australia's recreational fishery had its start when the first salmon were successfully reared at the Salmon Ponds.

Telecommunications history was made in 1888 when Australia's first trunk line call was connected from the Hobart GPO to the Bush Inn Hotel.

New Norfolk began to grow at a rapid rate in the twentieth century. Rich in soil and timber, the district's agricultural wealth was more easily exploited with the arrival of the railway, river steamers and hydro-electricity.

The Pioneer Woodware Company established a peg-making industry at New Norfolk in 1926, and in 1941 the first roll of Australian-made newsprint was produced at Boyer.

Australian Newsprint Mills led the Derwent Valley into its most prosperous era, almost doubling New Norfolk's size and population. Despite changes in ownership and workforce reductions, Boyer continues to supply the largest share of Australia's newsprint needs and is one of the state's biggest employers.

The end of Hydro-Electric Corporation dam construction and the closure of the Royal Derwent Hospital have sorely tested the Derwent Valley in the past decade.

The first years of the twenty-first century have seen the arrival of mainland investors big and small, a start on the redevelopment of the former hospital site and recognition of the tourism potential of the region.

Norfolk Island
Australian Territory

The Norfolk Island Flag

Norfolk Island adopted its own distinctive flag in 1980.
Central to the flag is a silhouette of one of Norfolk Island's most famous symbols – the Norfolk Island pine tree – which was first used on Norfolk Island's Great Seal, granted in 1856. The green stripes on each side symbolise Norfolk Island's abundant vegetation.

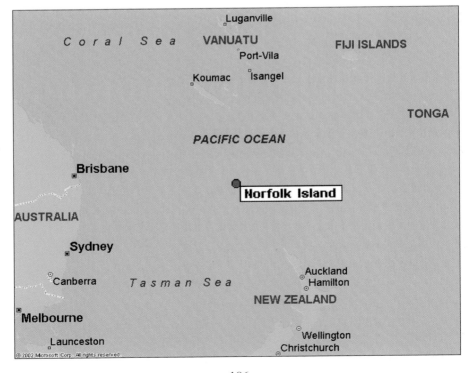

Luganville

C o r a l   S e a   **VANUATU**   **FIJI ISLANDS**
Port-Vila

Koumac   Isangel

TONGA

PACIFIC OCEAN

Brisbane

Norfolk Island

AUSTRALIA

Sydney

Auckland
Canberra   *T a s m a n   S e a*   Hamilton
NEW ZEALAND

Melbourne

Wellington
Launceston   Christchurch

186

Norfolk Island
Australian Territory
Pacific Ocean

Population: 1,900.
Administration: Administrator appointed by the Australian
Government and a Legislative Assembly of nine members.

Norfolk Island, an
Australian external territory
since 1913, lies 1,400 km
east of Australia in the
Pacific Ocean. A very green
island in a sea of blue.

Norfolk Island background
by Ian Hamilton McCowan (abridged)

Norfolk Island is a small fertile volcanic island lying in the Pacific
Ocean north-east of Sydney and north of Auckland with a couple of
smaller islands, the farther of which is 5 miles offshore.
The island was discovered by Captain Cook in 1774 and named, as
Cook had promised, after the Ninth Duchess of Norfolk.
The population is in part from the descendants of the Mutiny of the
Bounty, and further settlers from Australia, New Zealand and Great
Britain. The main income comes from tourists who are encouraged
by the duty free shopping as well as the great attraction of the
countryside – some 5 by 8 miles in extent.

There were three distinct settlements on Norfolk Island.
The first was 26 years of a convict settlement to 1814.
The second was another convict settlement of 36 years until 1855.
The third was the settling of the 194 mutineers' descendants in 1856,
who came from Pitcairn Island. These latter brought their individual
life style and language, a mixture of medieval English and Tahitian.

Norfolk Island came to the 1996 First Gathering of Norfolk

and Norwich Communities. They were the largest of the 19 delegations, but they came with a double intention. The first was the appreciation of the great potential in the formation of the "World Family".

The second was the celebration of the wedding of Alan and Judy
Kerr's son to a Norwich girl!

Nan and Fred Smith from the Island
during that momentous visit to
Norwich, England with the Norwich
Castle behind them, which began it
all...

Back to Norfolk Island, and the old Government House and prison remains from the days of the penal colony.

During our visit for the 2000 Gathering, Angela accepted the Norfolk and Norwich world map for the Island library.

And at the school, the principal, Ian McCowan, and one of his pupils at one of their famous "Fish Fry" picnics.

A walk in the wild

Agnes Hain who originated this unique facility also arranged for us to plant a tree in memory of our visit.

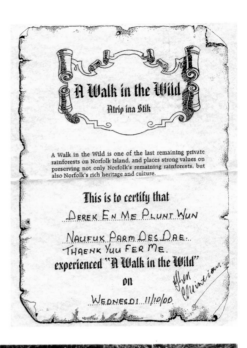

A Walk in the Wild
Ntrip ina Stik

A Walk in the Wild is one of the last remaining private rainforests on Norfolk Island, and places strong values on preserving not only Norfolk's remaining rainforests, but also Norfolk's rich heritage and culture.

This is to certify that

DEREK EN ME PLUNT WUN

NAUFUK PARM OES OAE.
THAENK YUU FER ME.

experienced "A Walk in the Wild"

on

WEDNESDI 11/10/00

While our guide was Tim Christian... left ... (related to that original mutineer on the good ship Bounty) with the excellent story of one of the "exported" prisoners being there because he shot an eminent Townsend in the backside as the latter ran away from an arranged duel over some lady's charms, and a diary written on banana skins....

And it's time to say farewell to Norfolk Island...

One final photograph of
me pointing to the landing
place of Captain Cook.

Manitoba Province Canada

The Manitoba Province Flag

The Official Flag of the Province of Manitoba is the Red Ensign, bearing the provincial Coat of Arms. This flag was given royal approval by Her Majesty Queen Elizabeth II in October 1965, and officially proclaimed on May 12, 1966.

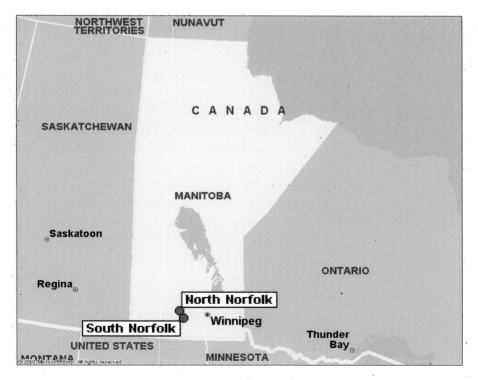

193

North Norfolk
Manitoba Province
Canada

Administration: Mayor and four
Councillors.
Population: 3,024.

The Rural Municipality of North Norfolk
is located in central Manitoba. North
Norfolk is easily accessible by the Trans
Canada Highway, which runs right
through the municipality. Provincial
Trunk Highway 34 and Provincial Roads 242, 350 and 352 also
service the municipality. The village of Macgregor, located just
off the Trans Canada Highway, is the largest urban centre in North
Norfolk (population 900). Austin, Sydney, Bagot and Rossendale are

The Annual Threshermen's
reunion and stampede is
held in July each year

other large communities in North Norfolk.
The municipality is situated in the rich
agricultural fields of Manitoba's central
plains region.
Agriculture is, understandably, a prominent
part of North Norfolk's economy. Yet
diversification in North Norfolk's economy
is beginning to take place.

With its proximity to the Trans Canada Highway, and being
approximately halfway between the major markets in Winnipeg
and Brandon, North Norfolk definitely has great potential for the
expansion or location of new businesses.

194

Canada's largest collection of operating vintage farm machinery from 1900 and beyond is located near Austin. The collection includes over 500 implements as well as a pioneer village with over 20 buildings.

Left: One of the modern farm "beasts", and right: the original pioneer house of the Muir family

My visit in 1995

The average temperatures are January –12C, April 10 C, July 26 C; yet when I visited in April the land was still hard frost and some of the roads showed remarkable frost damage. The unmade roads had an unfrozen layer that made driving "interesting".

Doug Lamb (centre) was my guide, seen here with Mr and Mrs Lyall who have an ostrich and dairy farm.
Ostriches lay big eggs!

Right: With my favourite administrators – Valerie Unrau and Olive Tunski

Left: the Council at the time of my visit: Mayor W. M.Wiebe and Secretary/Treasurer Lawrence Hart (centre), Councillors Clare Tarr and Darwin Crabbe (left), Herb Seaver and John Penner (right)

Right: the North Norfolk Municipal Offices.

My thanks to Clare Tarr for providing some of the photos on these pages.

Pearl and Nadine Dobbin representing both North and South Norfolk (hidden notice) and Manitoba at that first international gathering in 1996 in Norwich City, Norfolk County, England. The guard of honour was provided by the Girl Guides of Norfolk County.

The handsome, well dressed young man on the left is John Leader who farms in both South Norfolk, Manitoba and Suffolk, England.

196

The Legend of the White Horse

Early one summer in the 1690s, a band of Assiniboines was camped on the banks of the Assiniboine River, about ten miles west of present day Winnipeg. A young Cree brave from Lake Winnipegosis entered the Assiniboine camp and asked if he might marry the chief's daughter. The chief was offered a beautiful and spirited snow-white steed, a Blanco Diablo, which came from the famed breed in Mexico, and an agreement was reached.

This agreement upset a Sioux brave from Devil's Lake in North Dakota, also in love with the chief's daughter. He vowed to capture and torture his rival under the pretext of a reprisal for past wars. Aware of the danger, the Assiniboine chief saddled the white horse, and advised the couple to escape under cover of darkness.

When the Sioux learned of the escape, they followed, and eventually overtook the couple on the west bank of the Assiniboine River a few miles west of where the St. Francois-Xavier parish church now stands. Arrows killed both warrior and his bride.

The white horse escaped, and according to legend, continued to roam the neighbouring plains for many years. The Assiniboines believed that the spirits carried the horse to the spirit world where he was reunited with the Cree brave.

The aboriginal peoples named this land, where the white horse ran free, in honour of the powerful animal.

South Norfolk
Manitoba Province
Canada

Administration: Reeve and four Councillors.
Population: (outside the villages) 1,060.

The Municipality of South Norfolk is
nestled in the South Manitoba Prairie
– scenic beauty and fertile fields.
Canada became a country in 1867 and
Manitoba joined as a province in 1870.
From 1800 there were many settlers in this
welcoming land between the Assiniboine River (a river that winds so
much that a whole day's sailing might only traverse half a mile as the
crow flies!) and Tiger Hills. The homestead laws allowed the settlers
to receive a land title on 160 acres provided a three year tenancy had
achieved 15 acres of cultivated land plus a stable and shanty – this for
$1 an acre.

The municipality is one of the most
prosperous grain growing areas in Manitoba
and other crops include canola, flax, beans,
other cereals and sunflower. Hogs, dairy
and beef are the main livestock outputs.
The farms are mainly family farms and
Hutterite communities with some 50 to 150
individuals making a self-sufficient colony
with both church and school. There is also a
"First Nation" (native people's) reservation.

The scope for wildlife is large – extending from birds such as a partridge, to wolves and the occasional cougar or bear.

There are many community celebrations – Canada Day on July 1st with fireworks, and Remembrance Day on November 11th, while a "Gathering of Nations" in July and those many "Fall/Fowl Suppers" sound fascinating as well as "tasty"!

My visit in 1995

Jim Archer, Administrator (left), and John Steele, Reeve (right) with me during my visit in 1995

Treherne has the only educational facilities and the Collegiate (right) was presented with a video of Norwich, Norfolk, England, during my visit.

During my visit I was taken to this remarkable house, church, outhouse and well, totally made out of bottles by two retired farmers.

And then amongst the very many aspects there is the museum that has quite the largest collection of historical firearms.

Nadine and Pearl Dobbin, historians, represented both North and South Norfolks at the First Family Gathering in Norwich, England in 1996. (See photo on North Norfolk, Manitoba page). The Dobbins' history is a fascinating tale that deserves to be read in full. It is lodged in the new Norwich Library in the Forum, Norwich, England.

The Dobbin farm has an existing landmark of a grain elevator made out of logs that became jammed in the river.

I am happy to agree with Pearl and Nadine when they say "How lucky we are to call South Norfolk our home!"

Thank you for that fascinating story of your community – amongst the very best!

One further note is that at the Second World Gathering in 2000, on Norfolk Island, South Pacific, we had only the Manitoba flag and everyone wanted to know "Just where is South Norfolk?" I had much pride in telling them "just where"!

My Manitoba
(credit and resource Nadine Dobbin)

It's winter in Manitoba
And the gentle breezes blow
70 miles an hour and 52 degrees below
Oh, how I love my Manitoba
When the snow's up to your butt
You take a breath of winter air
Your nose freezes shut
Yes, the weather here is wonderful
I guess I'll hang around
I could never leave Manitoba
'Cause I'm frozen to the ground.

Ontario Province
Canada

The Ontario Province Flag

The Flag Act was proclaimed by the Ontario
Legislature on May 21, 1965. It declared the
requirements for the design of the Official Flag of
Ontario. The Canadian Red Ensign is used with
the Union Jack and the Ontario Shield of Arms.

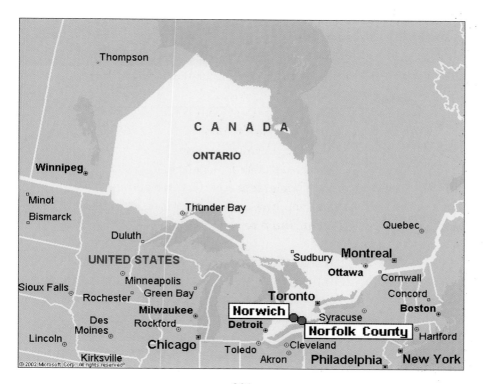

Norfolk County
Ontario Province
Canada

Administration: Mayor and nine Councillors.
Population: 61,000.

Norfolk County is located on the north
shore of Lake Eire. Port Dover, Long
Point, and many other communities
along the shoreline offer great holiday
destinations, be it on the water, fishing,
or exploring the countryside.
Simcoe is the administration centre
and largest town.

Simcoe Public Library

History of Norfolk County

Norfolk County is one of the oldest counties in Southern Ontario.
The majority of settlers who first came to Norfolk County were those
who were forced to vacate the American Colonies.

In 1776, 13 American states rebelled against Great Britain and those
that remained loyal to the Crown were forced to abandon all their
possessions. Some 3,000 settlers were welcomed and granted land by
the British government in acknowledgement of their sacrifice.
On January 1, 2001, the region of Haldimand Norfolk was dissolved
and made into two individual counties.

Views of Norfolk County, Ontario

Our thanks to Brenda Wood and Janet Woynarski for providing these photographs

The 2006 World Family Gathering

Norfolk County, Ontario are the hosts for the 2006 Norfolk and Norwich World Family Gathering which will be held to coincide with the annual County Fair and Horse Show.

Here are a few photographs to give you a feel of the event which lasts a week....

Norfolk Township (as was)
Haldiman Norfolk (as was)
Ontario Province, Canada

Despite the administrative changes that took out Norfolk Township in the new identification of Norfolk County, Ontario in 2001, I register the Norfolk Township delegation in fond memory of the excellent work they did to promote their township, their Ontario County and indeed their country, Canada. I have fond memories of my visit and being entertained in 1994, and their presence at the First World Family Gathering in 1996.

At the First Family Gathering in 1996

Mayor Hector Verhoeve and his delegation looked after by the Norwich City Town Crier and standing outside the old City Hall or Guildhall to give it its proper title – dating from 1420.

Mayor Hector Verhoeve with the Chief Executive of Norwich Union (again "as was", with a change at Norwich Union about the same time as that of the Township of Norfolk)

Amongst the many admired aspects of the Norfolk Township delegation was their vast distribution of Canadian flags! It was suggested that every third child of Norwich City, UK had one in that population of some 200,000!!!

Norwich Township were also the honoured guests of the British Legion Division of Norwich City, in company with those representatives of the Canadian Legion from their neighbouring Norwich Village, Oxford County, Ontario.

My visit in 1994

Right: John Backhouse, introduced by Hector, whose family I have since discovered has ancestral links back to the fifteenth century in England.

A farewell to Norfolk Township – Mayor Hector Verhoeve, with members of one of his Women's Institutes and his Chief Executive, in his seat of benevolent power – now part of the history of Norfolk County, Ontario.

(The Women's Institutes had their inception in Ontario and are now a power in England as well.)

Norwich Township
Oxford County
Ontario Province, Canada

Administration: Mayor and four Councillors.
Administraion Centre: Otterville.

There are four towns in the township:
Norwich, Burgesville and Otterville
(originally called South and North
Norwich), and Springford.

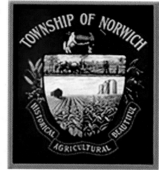

Township history
The township is rich with history,
taking shape in the year 1799 with
portions being settled by United
Empire Loyalists and Quakers. By
1807, a mill was operating in what is
now known as Otterville.
In 1864, Canada's first commercial
cheese factory went into operation. Mr
George Wilcox, known as the "father"
of free rural mail delivery, resided
within the township near the hamlet of
Springford. Many items of historical
significance reside at the Historical
Museum located in the village of
Norwich.

Right: Burgesville Library

207

Norwich Village
Oxford County
Ontario Province, Canada

Administration: Mayor and two Councillors.

My visit in 1994

Below left: Mayor John Heleniak on my visit in 1994, and right: just to show that the police in Norwich Village are very efficient…

The library is a remarkable building with a stained glass window that is rightly famous.

NORWICH & DISTRICT MUSEUM

RR #3 · Norwich, Ontario · N0J 1P0
(519) 863-3101 · Fax: (519) 863-2343

Left: Norwich and District Museum curators, Nancy and Jim Butler being presented with an old Norwich Union "fire mark". They were placed on the front of houses to certify that that house was insurance protected – otherwise the firemen would just watch it burn down! This was in the days when there were only privately run fire engines.

The real problem was that if the firemen attacked the fire then the contents were theirs and so it might be better not to have it insured?

Norwich and District Museum was originally the Quaker movement meeting house and represented that thriving community, and to this day the Friends are a vital part of Norwich Village.

As well as having a remarkable progression of agricultural inventions (the sit-down milking machine must have been only for extremely quiet cows!) there is an extremely efficient Historical Society.

One of the most remarkable facets of my all too short a visit in 1994 was the wonderful custom of the Canadian Legion giving the community a breakfast – via the organisation of Jacqueline and Lance Body.

The First Family Gathering in 1996

Norwich Village Canadian Legion and the Norwich and District Museum combined to come to Norwich England for that First World Gathering of Norfolk and Norwich communities in 1996 – then there were only 29 communities found. Since that time we now have 50 Norfolk and Norwich live communities – albeit some are very small from having been much more important in the early pioneering days.

And here – those pioneers in Norwich England, July 1996 to meet 30,000 Norwich and Norfolk citizens during the annual Lord Mayor's Parade. Front row Jacqueline Body and daughter holding the notice, and just behind wearing caps are Lance Body and his elder daughter. Every one was wearing the 'World Family' T-shirt. It was wonderful to have them with us and the British Legion gave them a right royal display and welcome as well!

Right: Royal British Legion's Henry Revell welcoming Lance Body of the Royal Canadian Legion

Jamaica

The Jamaican Flag

The Flag came into use on August 6, 1962, Jamaica's Independence Day. The Flag has a diagonal cross or saltire with four triangles in juxtaposition. The diagonal cross is gold and one-sixth of the length of the fly of the flag; the top and bottom triangles are in green; and the hoist and fly triangle are in black.

"The sun shineth, the land is green and the people are strong and creative" is the symbolism of the colours of the flag. Black depicts the strength and creativity of the people; gold, the natural wealth and beauty of sunlight; and green, hope and agricultural resources.

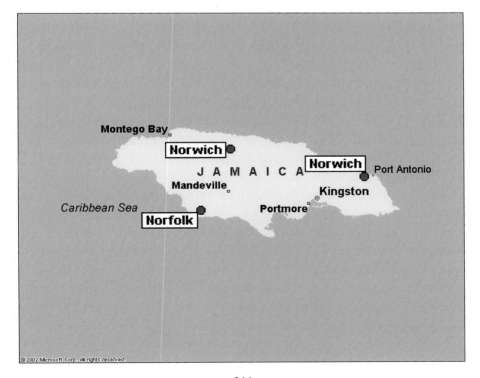

Norwich and Norwich Halt
Surrey County
Jamaica

Jamaica is, for me at least in my search for Norwich and Norfolks, still unexplored territory. Internet searches have provided only limited information. However, I was able to make contact with Elva McLean, Principal of the Norwich Primary School in Norwich, Surrey County, who has become one of the few school tutors to have supplied these interesting outlines (so many teachers in other schools are apparently too busy to be able to respond).

Norwich District is in the Parish of Portland and the Eastern County of Surrey. The name derives from Lord Norwich whose land it was, and it is some two miles west of Port Antonio. It is a rural community whose farm products are fruits of every kind and whose overall parish is the most famous in the world for its breadfruits. The first banana boat of the United Fruit Company docked in Port Antonio and this property adjacent to Norwich Primary School still has a reminder of the days of the sugar plantations via the copper sugar pots in which sugar was boiled.

Norwich is a seafront community with some of those famously beautiful Jamaican beaches.

The Norwich community is divided into two, with Norwich Halt being the bottom portion which includes the beaches. Norwich School and Norwich Guest House are in Top Norwich. Some of the roads are asphalted while others are partially rough, strong and bad. Water is supplied by pipes via a dam/resevoir while there are rivers supplying water for domestic use.

Electricity is a 95 per cent resource and there are many clubs and associations, with a particularly strong Youth and Community club – currently the football champions!
Whilst telephone services are available throughout, the use of computer and fax facilities is yet in small supply.

We have found references to another Norwich and a Norfolk in Jamaica, but as yet have no further information....

Norwich, St Ann Parish, Middlesex County
Location: 18°21'N, 77°25'W

Norfolk, St Elizabeth Parish, Cornwall County
Location: 17°53'N, 77°40' W

North Island
New Zealand

The New Zealand Flag

The New Zealand Flag is blue with the flag of the UK in the upper hoist-side quadrant representing its connection with the United Kingdom, and four red five-pointed stars edged in white centered in the outer half of the flag; the stars laid out to represent the Southern Cross constellation.

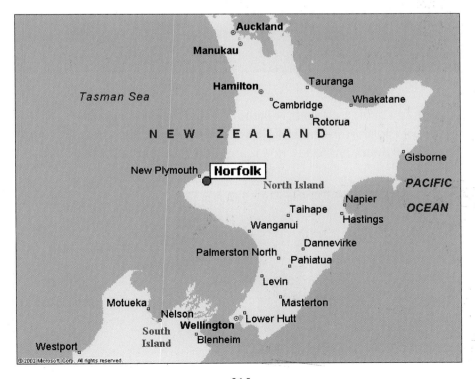

215

Norfolk
Taranaki Province
New Zealand

Norfolk is a small farming area in the Taranaki Province. It is in fact, Rural District 8 in Inglewood. It consists of a school country hall and tennis courts, not to forget two swimming pools.

Mount Taranaki in one guise

Mount Taranaki being shy!

Mount Taranaki, a domant volcano dominates the views in this corner of the North Island of New Zealand. Once the whole area was heavily forested, but today it is mainly the lush green grass of dairy farms.

Bob and Joyce Wilson with the Mayor of New Plymouth (the area capital) Claire Stewart holding the "family plaque" as presented to Norfolk School.

The World Family of Norfolk and Norwich plaque presented at the school, and the young ones – who are the educated ones!

The school has a long history, as commemorated with this plaque...

Area background

Immigrants from the English Devon area came in 1841, and Polish immigrants in 1876. These were all the real pioneers and working hard all their lives, the forests were cleared and railways evolved. The oil and gas industries have made a huge impact since 1970 so that roads and busy New Plymouth Airport have made this a far less remote region than it used to be.

Norfolk Road now has an update airstrip for gliding and it was here that the New Zealand Sky Diving Championship was hosted.

1996 was the first ever World Family gathering in Norwich, Norfolk County, England and the delegation from New Zealand were a great joy.

Joyce Wilson and Lois Tidswell were particularly happy to have the plaque which memorised Lois's husband's visit to Norwich England in 1996.

And then the "central help organisation" visited Norwich, Norfolk, England. Here Joyce and Bob pictured with the 1,000 year old Norwich Castle behind them.

Certainly one of the real community events during my visit to New Zealand was that family party held at the Wilsons!

My contribution to New Zealand and my "discoverer" of Norfolk, NZ: daughter Jo becoming a Watson.

And here she is with Colin Watson, her first born and a true New Zealander!